SEA
TURTLES

The Watchers' Guide

by M. Timothy O'Keefe

Foreword by
Peter C.H. Pritchard

Larsen's Outdoor Publishing

SEA TURTLES

ISBN 0-936513-47-0

Library of Congress 95-075545

Published by:

LARSEN'S OUTDOOR PUBLISHING
2640 Elizabeth Place
Lakeland, FL 33813
(941) 644-3381
(941) 644-3288 fax

PRINTED IN THE UNITED STATES OF AMERICA

2 3 4 5 6 7 8 9 10

ACKNOWLEDGMENTS

I would like to thank all those who helped make this book possible, especially Peter C.H. Pritchard, one of the world's foremost sea turtle experts, who really has far more important things to do in life than correct my manuscript. His photographs also add immeasurably to this book.

Also thanks to Beth Morford of the Office of Protected Species, Department of Environmental Protection; Wendell Simpson at Canaveral National Seashore; Milda Simonitis of the Gumbo Limbo Nature Center; Melody Bell at the Museum of Discovery and Science in Ft. Lauderdale; Larry Wood of the Marinelife Center of Juno Beach; Norma Jeanne Body of the Nature Conservancy; Debbie Fritz-Quincy of the Hobe Sound Nature Center; Dr. J.R. Wilcox, Florida Power & Light; Sidney Love of John U. Lloyd Beach State Recreation Area; John Fillyaw at J.D. MacArthur Beach State Park; Ronald Johns and Terry O'Toole at Sebastian Inlet State Recreation Area; Dean Bagley of Orlando; Eve Haverford at Turtle Time; Tina Brown and Richie Moretti at Hidden Harbour Motel, Marathon; Dr. Jean Mortimer of the Caribbean Conservation Corporation; and various staff of The Florida Aquarium in Tampa.

SEA TURTLES

DEDICATION

To all those trying to save our sea life.

Peter Pritchard photo

"There are two times in the life of a sea turtle when a zoologist can count on making contact with it: when it hatches, and when the female goes ashore to nest. Everything else is done away off somewhere out of sight, and has to be reconstructed by deduction from fragments of observation."

Archie Carr, The Sea Turtle

5

SEA TURTLES

FOREWORD

Sometimes, we who work for conservation of nature find ourselves ambivalent about the outcome of some of our activities. For example, our profession is to preserve nature by whatever means we can. At times we feel inspired to write about the places that are so awe-inspiring that they move the spirit, and we invite those who do not yet share our value system to do so by both reading and by experiencing earth's spectacular natural places and phenomena. Surely, we instinctively feel, a populace whose soul is inspired by the wonders of nature, and that is concerned about the fate of endangered species, is fundamentally and absolutely better than a nation of Philistines.

And it is so. But is does have a down side, too. An increasingly nature-conscious populace places demands upon the more scenic National and State Parks that their founders never imagined. Our own personal, favorite "quiet places" also become public once we write about them, and solitude celebrated and publicized may well, and quickly, become solitude despoiled, existing only in the memory.

A pair of stuffed hawksbill turtles on sale in Saipan.

A further paradox is that, in working for conservation, we are expressing a belief in the value not only of nature, but of personal freedom, of the right to enjoy wilderness, and to wander until one is beyond the reach of *Homo sapiens* and his influence, his roads, his regulations, and his rubbish. But what do we find ourselves actually doing? In order to protect nature, we become, not cutters, but makers of red tape, lobbyists for more, not less, legislation, and proponents of ever more government involvement in our everyday lives, with the proliferation of regulations (and taxation!) that this inevitably entails.

It is sad but it is probably unavoidable. Complex societies require complex administration. And nowhere are the dilemmas more in the forefront than in the field of conservation of the great, awe-inspiring sea turtles, the heroes of this book by my old friend Tim O'Keefe.

We all like turtles, and many of us love them. There are unenlightened souls among us who would still sleep at night if snakes or crocodiles were to disappear, but no one would wish such a fate upon our unthreatening shelled colleagues, the turtles. Moreover, the ability of turtles, marine and freshwater, to exist alongside ourselves, both figuratively and literally, is impressive.

Not only do snapping turtles and painted turtles manage to live within the confines of some of the largest cities in the eastern United States, but the personal propinquity of sitting quietly beside a nesting sea turtle for a hour or more, hearing her breathing and quiet sighing in the blackness of the night but provoking no fear on the part of either the observer or the observed, is a unique experience. How many other wild creatures, as big as or bigger than ourselves, can we commune with in this way, so close and for so long, without them either taking off at high speed -- or having us for lunch?

This book not only gives an excellent overview of sea turtle life, it also provides the specifics of appropriate personal conduct and behavior for human beings on turtle nesting beaches. Despite my internal agonizing and personal dilemmas about people ultimately ''loving nature to death,'' I believe that everyone in Florida with even a scrap of interest in nature should, sooner or later, watch a turtle nesting. Turtles nest in the summer months on many of our beaches, but they prefer those within the central section of the Atlantic coast--Broward to Brevard.

It is true that the very attractiveness of the spectacle means that the demand for places on many of the more popular organized ''turtle walks'' is extreme. But put your name down nonetheless. You will not be unmoved by what you see, and you will never forget the experience. And, if

SEA TURTLES

you follow the guidelines that Tim O'Keefe patiently describes at the back of this book, you will be able to enjoy the turtle-watching experience without, unwittingly, making life just a little harder for the turtle itself. Then, once home, you will be a permanent defender of the embattled sea turtles. Their travails, at the hands of shrimpers and other fishers, beachfront developers, poachers, and others are such that they need all the help and protection they can get.

Peter C. H. Pritchard, Ph.D.
Florida Audubon Society

ABOUT THE AUTHOR

M. Timothy O'Keefe, writer/photographer for more than 30 years, is also the author of Larsen's Outdoor Publishing's best-selling <u>Manatees, Our Vanishing Mermaids</u>. His articles and photographs have appeared in numerous publications worldwide, including National Geographic Society books, Time-Life Books, Rodale's Scuba Diving, SCUBA Times, Diving & Snorkeling, Caribbean Travel & Life, Newsweek, Travel & Leisure, and more. He is an award-winning author of <u>Diving to Adventure</u> and co-author of <u>Fish & Dive Florida & The Keys</u> and <u>Fish & Dive the Caribbean, Vol. 1</u>, listed in the Resource Directory at the back of this book.

Tim holds a PhD from the University of North Carolina at Chapel Hill and is a professor in the School of Communication at the University of Central Florida in Orlando, where he established the journalism program. He is a member of the Outdoor Writers Association of America (OWAA), the Society of American Travel Writers (SATW), American Society of Journalists and Authors (ASJA) and a past president of the Florida Outdoor Writers Association (FOWA).

SEA TURTLES

CONTENTS

SEA TURTLES

INTRODUCTION

Since most endangered species live in remote, out-of-the-way places, it's rare for the average person to view endangered or threatened animals roaming freely on their home turf. Sea turtles, however, are a remarkable exception.

From May to September, female turtles of up to 1.300 pounds ponderously crawl ashore night after night on beaches throughout the Southeast. Each turtle has the same single-minded goal: to bury her eggs in a nest and return to the sea before daylight.

Witnessing a turtle is an unforgettable lesson in species survival.

Until recently, only researchers, scientists and poachers usually saw the nesting process. But new public awareness programs are allowing more of us to witness this spectacle.

Few things are more memorable (or emotional) than watching a sea turtle complete the nesting process. Raccoons may dig out and destroy her eggs while she is still depositing them, but an egg-laying turtle perseveres nonetheless, rarely stopping for any reason.

It's as if she is the only remaining survivor of her race, and that her successful nesting is the only thing that matters in the world.

SEA TURTLES

For most people, the sight and the sounds of the nesting process are unforgettable, an experience that never completely leaves them.

Sea turtles nest only on subtropical and tropical beaches. Science currently recognizes eight sea turtle species belonging to six genera. Five of the eight species nest in the United States. They are the loggerhead *(Caretta caretta)*; the green turtle *(Chelonia mydas)*; the leatherback *(Dermochelys coriacea)*; the hawksbill *(Eretmochelys imbricata)*; and the rarest of all sea turtles, the Kemp's ridley *(Lepidochelys kempi)*.

Sea turtle nesting grounds in the United States extend from Texas through Florida along the Gulf of Mexico, and from the Florida Keys to Virginia on the Atlantic Coast.

The heaviest concentration of nesting turtles is on Florida's Atlantic Coast, from New Smyrna to Boca Raton with the maximum density in southern Brevard County. This area accounts for 80 percent of the nests seen on the entire U.S. East Coast. On the Gulf Coast, most nests are also laid in Florida, between Pinellas and Monroe Counties.

This book is intended to provide basic background information on the identification and life cycle of the marine turtle species that nest in U.S. coastal waters. Although the nesting rituals are very parallel, the different species of sea turtles are actually quite dissimilar in terms of diet, behavior and habitat preference. And, once you know what to look for, it is also quite easy to tell the various sea turtles apart.

The guide also identifies and describes the turtle watching programs open to the public. A word of caution: turtle watches are incredibly popular, and the number of people allowed to participate on any one night is quite limited. Advance reservations are mandatory.

So are long pants, long sleeve shirts and insect repellent!

■

1

■

LIFE AND TIMES OF THE SEA TURTLES

Turtles as a group are believed to have first appeared on earth about 200 million years ago. All turtles are believed to have evolved from the cotylosaurs, a group of early reptiles from which not only all living reptiles, but even mammals and birds, evolved.

Turtles have not changed very much in a long, long time. For instance, the turtles of the Triassic period (175,000,000 years ago) already had the same fundamental characteristics as the turtles we see today. The earliest sea turtle fossils date back about 150,000,000 years, to a time when vast shallow seas covered much of the earth.

There are more than 250 different turtle species living today. Many are nature's version of an unstoppable tank. All turtles enjoy the benefit of a bony shell that encloses their vital organs and into which their head, limbs and tail can usually be withdrawn. The shells of some turtles are so strong they can endure the weight of a 200-pound man without damage.

Like alligators, crocodiles and other reptiles, the activity level of a sea turtle is related to the temperature. (The

SEA TURTLES

notable exception is the leatherback. When it's too hot or too cold, sea turtles tend to be inactive.

Sea Turtle Adaptations

Sea turtles adapted in several specialized ways because of their watery habitat. As the name implies, sea turtles live in the ocean, although they may sometimes be found in brackish water or the estuaries of big rivers.

Their forelimbs are sleek and paddle-like to propel them swiftly through the ocean. Their shells also became more streamlined and less box-like than many land species. But in gaining these aquatic advantages, sea turtles also lost the ability to retract their heads inside their shells for protection.

Over the course of evolution, many reptiles have increased their number of vertebrae to provide greater motion or speed. Turtles have tended to go in the opposite direction. They have just eight neck vertebrae, often with highly mobile or flexible joints, followed by the ten completely immovable dorsal vertebrae, fused below the midline of the back shell (or carapace). There are also a variable number of sacral and tail vertebrae.

Because they spend almost their entire lives in the water, sea turtles developed with more than just lungs for breathing. They are able to exchange oxygen and carbon dioxide with the surrounding water thanks to extensive capillary vascularization in the cloacal cavity, and the buccal cavity. By circulating water in these cavities and also reducing their metabolism dramatically, sea turtles can stay submerged from between 40 minutes to five hours if they are not active and the water is not too warm.

Sea turtles do not have teeth. Their bird-like beaks and jaws are quite powerful, able to crush, tear or chew food with little problem. Like all reptiles, sea turtles lack

Sea turtles lack teeth. Instead, they have bird-like beaks and powerful jaws.

external ears. Instead, the sea turtle eardrum is covered over by skin.

The largest turtle living today is a sea turtle, the Atlantic leatherback *(Dermochelys coriacea).* Giant leatherbacks have been reported to grow up to 1,300 pounds and measure eight feet from the tip of one flipper to that of the other, but this is uncommon. An even larger marine turtle, *Archelon,* once lived in North America but it is now extinct. The ocean it once occupied is now the Great Plains of the Central

SEA TURTLES

United States. By comparison, the largest living land tortoises weigh only slightly more than 500 pounds.

Turtles have a reputation for being among the slowest animals on earth thanks to Aesop's fable of ''The Tortoise and the Hare.'' But that tale was about a tortoise, a term that technically refers only to land dwellers. Many tortoises do move very slowly. For instance, the gopher tortoise found in Florida and much of the Southeast has been clocked from 0.13 to 0.30 miles per hour. Some forms of tropical vegetation almost seem to grow faster than tortoises move.

Sea turtles are a speedy contrast. In their watery environment, they are capable of tremendous bursts of speed that human swimmers can only envy. Divers who attempt to swim with a sea turtle in a futile attempt to photograph it normally end up with nothing but tail shots. Green turtles are said to swim as fast as 30 feet (10 meters) per second!

From tagging studies done with green turtles (perhaps the most studied species), it's known that greens are capable of swimming 300 miles in just 10 days. How much of each 24-hour day a turtle might actually swim on such a marathon is not known.

Courtship and Nesting

Sea turtles are often seen far from any shore, and some of these world travelers seem to grow a second shell--of barnacles. Except for a few remote Pacific beaches, where they may bask, male sea turtles spend 100 percent of their lives in the ocean. Female turtles have only one need of the land: to deposit their eggs.

Although hatchlings do cooperate in emerging from the nest, afterwards it's every turtle for itself since parents provide no care at all. As adults, sea turtles seem to have

The leatherback is the largest turtle in the world. Peter Pritchard

Turtles tend to be solitary creatures. Conditions at this green turtle farm are extremely unnatural.

Radio tracking devices have been used for several decades to monitor turtle migrations. Peter Pritchard

very little need for each other, either, since they are solitary creatures most of the time.

The only true social interaction is said to occur during courtship and mating. Males test a female's receptivity by nuzzling her head and gently biting her neck and flippers.

Reluctant females may fold their hind flippers together. Greens have been reported adopting a refusal position in the water by facing the male vertically with her limbs widespread.

If a female is willing, the male mounts her and grips the front of her shell with his forelimbs and curls his tail under her shell. Mating may take place on the ocean bottom, the surface or in open water. Mating occurs about 30 days before the females begin nesting. The early season matings will fertilize the whole season's eggs.

Mating couples sometimes have an audience of one or more ''attendant'' males who bite the flippers and tail of the successful male. The rivals may even try to dislodge

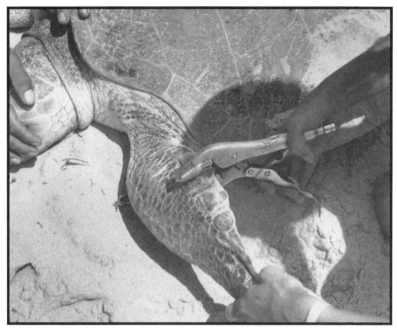

Tagging studies show females do return to the same beaches over and over once they start to nest. Peter Pritchard

him. The mating male may remain in place despite suffering what must be painful injury.

In some parts of the world, native fishermen take advantage of the intense male mating drive by floating large wooden "decoy" turtles, which are attached to the boat by ropes. Fishermen capture the males when they attempt to mount the decoys.

Navigational Abilities

It's a common assumption that sea turtles nest on the same beach where they hatched. The late Archie Carr, one of the world's foremost experts of sea turtle ecology, certainly believed this. He describes one green turtle coming ashore as pushing "her head this way and that with a darting motion less like the slow movement you expect of a green turtle than like a lizard or snake, then lower her head and nose the hard, wet beach as if to smell for telltale signs of generations of ancestors there before her.'' (from The Sea Turtle, p. 21).

The mystery is how a female turtle locates the beach of her birth. Certainly it's far more than a matter of sight.

Consider the situation from a sea turtle's point of view. Floating at the surface, she is unable to raise her head even as high as a human swimmer can. Furthermore, although sea turtles can see quite well underwater, they are extremely near-sighted in the air.

So how do turtles swim hundreds of miles from shore, yet find their way back to the same beaches year after year? We do not know.

It's been suggested that turtles may follow a special taste or smell that is unique to each area of the ocean or coastline. The brain area that governs a sea turtle's sense of smell is very well developed. Sea turtles also have a highly magnetic substance in their brains which might enable them to detect, or navigate by, the earth's magnetic fields. Therefore, it's quite possible sea turtles may use a combination of senses to form their natural guidance system.

Ironically, despite all the speculation about turtle navigation, it's still only an assumption that adult sea turtles return to the very same beaches where they were born. Incontrovertible scientific proof of this belief does not yet exist. The reason: no feasible tagging method has yet been developed that endures from the time the tiny hatchlings rush to the sea until they emerge years later as the vastly larger nesting adults.

But tagging has shown that females do return to the same beaches over and over once they mature and start to nest. Tagging has also disclosed that the same female may

Taking off for parts unknown: where do the hatchlings go?

nest between two and a six times a season (even 10 times for a leatherback) and that she may lay her eggs only every second or third year. A common misconception is that females tend to deposit their eggs around the time of the full moon. The theory is that the full moon creates a higher tide, which in turns will better hide the nesting trails. Excellent logic, but it doesn't appear to be true. Turtles nest during all phases of the moon.

Indeed, with cycles of 10 to about 17 days between nestings, a nesting with the full moon on one occasion will be followed by a very reduced moon--or no moon at all--the next time.

Where Do All The Hatchlings Go?

Turtle eggs incubate for about 60 days. The hatchlings normally break out of the nest and make their mad dash for the sea at night. Not all of the turtles may emerge simultaneously, but the last (except for handicapped or imperfect ones) are usually gone within 48 hours of the first wave.

If a hatchling reaches the hot surface sand during the day, it will usually not emerge any farther, but will wait until night before making its final exit. The daytime heat could be fatal to a hatchling, especially if it did not find the sea immediately. The cool of the night is safer for the dash to the sea; also, the cover of darkness will foil some predators, but not cats and crabs or a few birds, like night herons.

The first year of life is a precarious one for marine turtles since their small size makes them easy prey for birds and fish.

It's easy to believe that the young turtles are very much aware of this: they totally disappear their first year of life. Scientists agree that where the hatchlings go until they reach eight to 10 inches in length is a mystery worthy of Sherlock Holmes. Leatherbacks and olive ridleys are rarely seen until they mature.

One popular idea is that the hatchlings go out to sea and live in the driftlines where seaweed and other debris float in long streaks on the surface. Driftlines (which have long been recognized by sportsmen as rich fishing areas because of the concentrated food and cover) form when ocean currents meet and sink.

Turtles cannot dive more than a few inches when first hatched, so the drift theory during that first "lost year" appears quite probable. Interestingly, young turtles also react more to vibrations in the water than they do sound. And when they sleep floating on the surface, they keep their flippers out of the water by folding them over on their back.

SEA TURTLES

Wherever they may go as youngsters, sea turtles spend their juvenile and subadult years in bays, estuaries and shallow coastal waters. At maturity, they travel to traditional feeding grounds to join other adults. Depending on locale, feeding and nesting areas may sometimes be hundreds of miles apart.

How long do sea turtles live? That's another question still be pondered. Although they are believed to live for a fairly long time, to 80 or 100 years or more, no accepted method has yet been devised for inspecting sea turtles and determining their age. But research continues: there are indications, for example, that the long bones will form annual ''growth'' rings that, up to a point, can be counted.

■

2

■

HOW TO IDENTIFY
SEA TURTLES

With the exception of the leatherback, different species of sea turtles often appear very similar at first glance since their shells all seem to have the same basic design and shape.

However, the top (carapace) and bottom (plastron) vary considerably between species. So do the number and shape of the horny plates (scutes) that cover the carapace.

Consider the back of a sea turtle as a kind of blueprint for each species; it takes only a few minutes to learn how to read one.

Several scientific terms are used to distinguish the different parts of a shell. The foremost plate of a carapace-- the small, midline one above the neck--is the nuchal. The row of plates along the median line or midline of the carapace are the vertebrals, which lie directly above the vertebrae.

Adjacent to the neurals on each side of the shell are the costal plates. The costals are surrounded by the marginal scutes which form the carapace's outer edge. Beneath the scutes are the actual bones of the shell, which fuse with the dorsal vertebrae (backbone) and the ribs.

SEA TURTLES

The Loggerhead

This is the most common species of nesting turtle on Florida beaches. Florida alone has close to 90 percent of the nestings in the U.S. Loggerheads also nest farther north than any other species, with one isolated record from as far north as Ocean City, New Jersey. Outside of Florida, the most important nesting sites are on the offshore islands of Georgia and South Carolina. There is no nesting on the Pacific coast of the U.S., although the Mexican Pacific has important beaches for several sea turtle species.

The loggerhead is named for its large head, which may be up to ten inches across. Such a large head is partly due to its heavy jaw musculature and its hard-shelled diet, which includes clams, conch, barnacles and other mollusks. Loggerheads also eat crabs, shrimp, jellyfish and sea grasses.

The loggerhead's large, reddish brown shell is distinctive in that it has five or more costal plates on each side of the neurals. The underside (plastron) is yellow. Three pairs of scutes (called inframarginal scutes) separate the large plastron scutes from the marginal scutes at the shell's edge. All loggerhead scutes are without pores. In young and half-grown animals, the vertebral scutes are raised or keeled, like tiny mountain ridges and peaks.

In addition, two pairs of large scales called prefrontals are located on the top of the head between the eyes and the nostrils. Each of the loggerhead's forelimbs has two claws. The male has a much longer tail which enables him to grasp the female during mating.

Loggerheads mature between the ages of 20 and 30 years. Adults rarely weigh more than 350 pounds, although giants of up to 500 pounds are occasionally reported. The adult carapace attains a length of between 35 and 42 inches long, but the Mediterranean nesting turtles (in Turkey and

CARAPACES

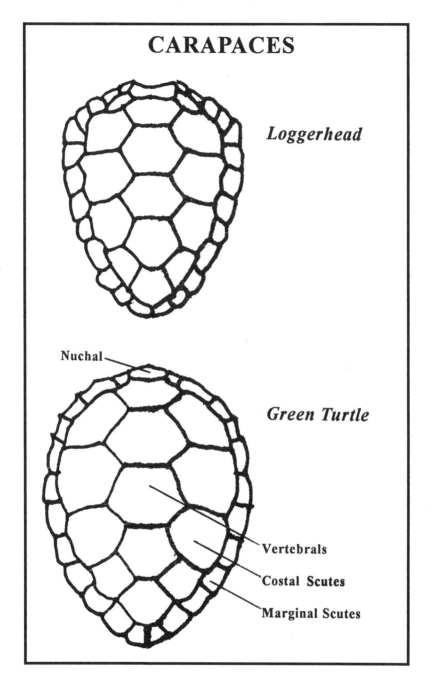

Loggerhead

Nuchal

Green Turtle

Vertebrals

Costal **Scutes**

Marginal Scutes

PLASTRONS

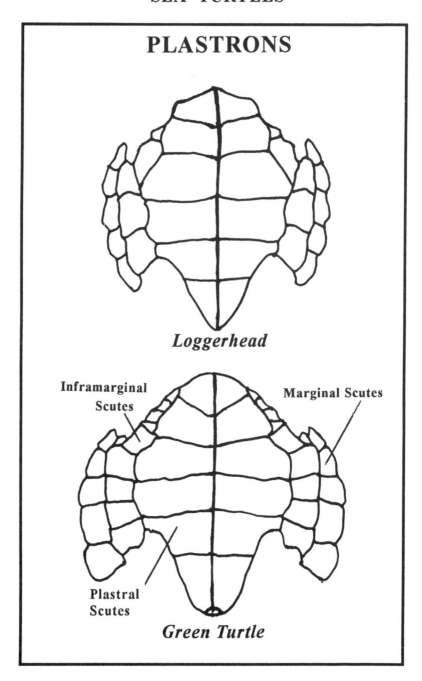

Loggerhead

Green Turtle

Inframarginal Scutes

Marginal Scutes

Plastral Scutes

Greece) are much smaller. Loggerheads are believed to be capable of reproduction for as long as 30 years.

Loggerhead meat was never popular commercially. It is tougher than green turtle because it has more sinew. Further, loggerheads aren't as meek as greens when it comes to defending themselves. They have been known to grab and bite people.

Loggerhead nesting begins in spring, extending from late April to September. An average clutch consists of about 100 eggs. The eggs incubate for about 60 days before producing two-inch hatchlings that weigh only 3/5 of an ounce.

After nesting, the females travel long distances to their feeding grounds, which may be as far away as Cuba or the Dominican Republic. Ironically, there are also seemingly excellent nesting beaches in those regions. Why the loggerheads commute to the United States is anyone's guess. In the past, when turtles were more abundant in the Caribbean, the beaches there may have been fully utilized by greens and hawksbills.

Green Turtles

Green turtles are not named for their external coloration, which is commonly olive-brown with dark streaks, but from the color of their body fat. Compared to the loggerhead's five, the green has only four costal plates on each side adjoining the vertebral series. The plates do not overlap (except very slightly in the very young). The edge of the carapace is smooth or slightly wavy. A small but important distinguishing mark is the single pair of elongate prefrontal scales on the upper snout; most other species have these divided into four prefrontal scutes. The underside (plastron) tends to be white in the young and yellowish in adults. The jaws, which are used primarily for grazing on sea grasses,

SEA TURTLES

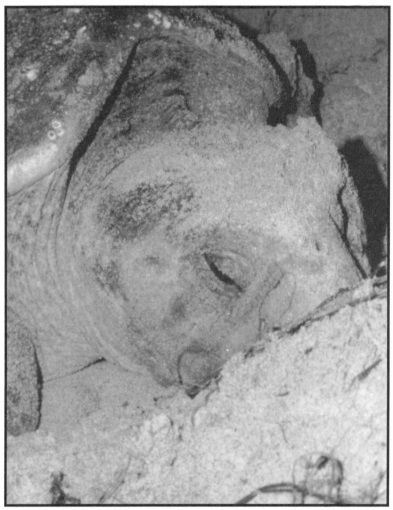

The loggerhead is named for its large head.

are not as beak-like as the loggerhead's, and have serrated surfaces. The paddle-shaped flippers each have only a single claw.

At one time, green turtles were among the most abundant of the sea turtles, found literally in the millions between

The green turtle, whose soup has long been considered a delicacy.

North Carolina and Argentina. In the Pacific, the related "black turtles" still range as far south as Chile and occasionally as far north as Alaska.

Green turtle stocks were severely depleted because of the quality of their meat (tasty and tender) and the delicious soup made from their fat. The intense vulnerability of the nesting females and their eggs was the real problem.

Greens average slightly larger than loggerheads and weigh over 350 pounds. The largest are in the South

SEA TURTLES

Sea turtles like this green turtle are far speedier than any land tortoise.

Atlantic (Ascension Island and the Guianas) where weights of over 500 pounds and carapaces up to 48-inches long are not unusual.

Greens have the most unusual diet of all sea turtles. As hatchlings and juveniles they dine happily on jellyfish. However, once a green's shell attains between eight to 10 inches, the animal begins consuming sea grasses and algae on shallow flats. As adults, greens are nearly exclusive vegetarians, the only adult sea turtles which are, eating sea grasses, sea weed and the occasional jellyfish, too.

Greens tend to have favorite hangouts under rocks and coral ledges in relatively shallow waters. They prefer to graze on the youngest plant growth available, possibly because these are both more tender and also highest in

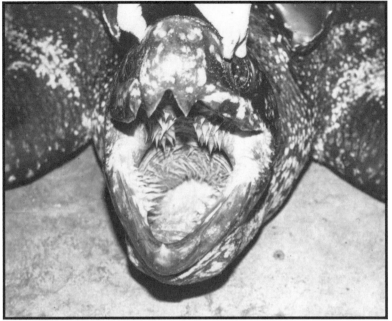

The leatherback's mouth and throat have numerous spines to retain its favorite food, jellyfish. Peter Pritchard

protein. Still, this is a low protein diet overall and growth is slow. Greens may not mature until 20 or 30 years of age.

In some regions, greens appear to mate very close to the nesting beaches; in other regions, mating and nesting may occur hundreds of miles apart. Hatchlings measure about two inches in length.

On the Atlantic coast, greens almost never nest farther north than Florida. Nesting occurs from June through late September. The annual nest count is quite limited, reflecting their endangered status. Normally, between 500 to 2,800 green nests are recorded each season on Florida's east coast, mostly between Volusia and Broward Counties.

There are hopeful signs that the North Atlantic green turtle population may be increasing. In the U.S., the nesting count is on the upturn. Furthermore, a resident year-round population of immature greens at Mosquito Lagoon near Titusville is steadily growing. Mosquito Lagoon has been suggested as the most northerly winter range of the green turtle. Even so, this is an area that also undergoes hard freezes in occasional years.

Besides the resident population at Mosquito Lagoon, the number of green turtles nesting in the Gulf of Mexico has begun to increase. In 1994, 29 nests were located, most in Sarasota and Charlotte counties, where there had not been a report of a green turtle nest for almost a decade. Across the Gulf, at Rancho Nuevo, Mexico, a green turtle nesting population has built up in recent years.

Green turtles are the true ocean migrators. Their incredible homing and nesting instincts are best illustrated by the green turtles that feed off the coast of Brazil. To nest, they travel east 1,400 miles through open water to reach tiny five-mile wide Ascension Island.

How do they find it? Why do they journey so far? The answers: as yet unknown.

Leatherback Turtles

Leatherbacks are the Godzillas of the turtle world. Largest of all sea turtles, they grow up to 1,300 pounds with shell length up to six feet. They also do things of which no other sea turtle--or any species of reptile--is capable.

Leatherbacks are able to dive to below 3,300 feet deep, possibly the greatest depth for any air breathing vertebrate. Only the sperm whale and elephant seals may match or exceed the leatherback's deep dives.

What draws a leatherback so deep? Possibly jellyfish. It seems unlikely that such a powerful and large animal would subsist on almost nothing but jellyfish, but that does appear to be the case. A leatherback's mouth is specially adapted

The leatherback is the most streamlined sea turtle. Peter Pritchard

for a jellyfish diet. First, the turtle sucks in its food by expanding its throat. To retain the soft food, the mouth contains numerous stiff, three-inch spines that point backward and the six-foot esophagus is lined with backward-pointing spines. The razor-sharp, notched jaws are also well adapted for cutting and holding soft prey like jellyfish. However, the examination of stomach contents indicates the leatherback diet in some locales may be more varied.

Jellyfish, which are mostly water, are poor suppliers of energy on a per-pound basis. A hungry young leatherback may eat double its weight in jellyfish in a day, and these are most abundant in regions far away from the tropical nesting grounds. Leatherbacks have been known to "graze" as far north as Labrador and Alaska. Sometimes, a good jellyfish must be hard to find: leatherbacks have been recorded feeding as far as 3,100 miles from their nesting grounds.

CARAPACES

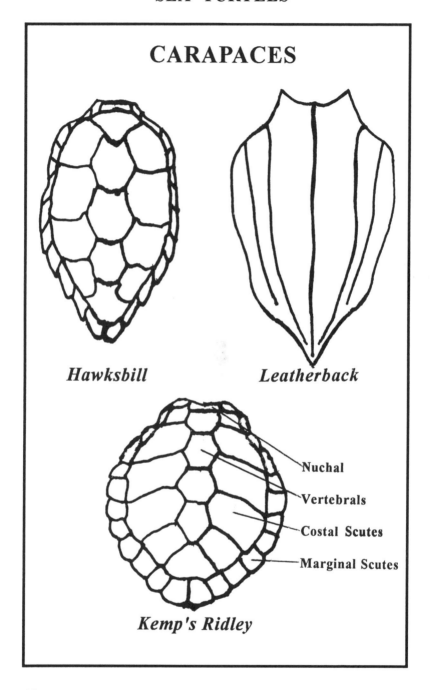

Hawksbill   *Leatherback*

Nuchal

Vertebrals

Costal Scutes

Marginal Scutes

Kemp's Ridley

40

Like many deep ocean inhabitants, leatherbacks are normally dark on the top (though some have heavy white spotting) and white on the bottom. Except when close to their nesting areas, they are typically found in water at least 150 feet deep.

Leatherbacks are the only sea turtles without a hard shell. Instead, their shell is rubbery or leather-like and is permeated by large quantities of oil. This oil most likely has some function in avoiding the "bends" on deep dives. It may also help with insulation, allowing leatherbacks to remain active and sustain a body temperature as high as 75 degrees in water as cold as 43 degrees, something a reptile is not supposed to be able to do.

The body temperature of reptiles is supposed to approximate the water or air temperature around them. Forty-three degrees would put almost every other known species of reptile into a state of extreme lethargy, to say the least. However, scientists have been able to measure and determine that leatherbacks are indeed different from other reptiles. Leatherbacks possess the remarkable ability to regulate their own body temperature, which allows them to maintain activity in very cold conditions.

More than any other sea turtle, the leatherback is built for speed. It has powerful front flippers but lacks the normal claws; the leatherback is the only sea turtle without them. Its head, carapace and lower shell all join smoothly together like a seamed barrel. The carapace also has seven streamlined ridges (or keels) that extend the length of its back that makes it easier to track through the water at high speeds.

Leatherbacks may never have been numerous enough to exploit on a large scale, not even for their oil. However, the oil has been used for medicinal purposes in several parts of the world, and for boat sealant. Today, there are an

The Kemp's ridley is the rarest and most endangered of all sea turtles. Peter Pritchard

estimated 70,000 to 115,000 breeding female leatherbacks throughout the world, possibly increasing in the Atlantic but dropping in the East Pacific.

Leatherbacks nest in Florida from April through July. Mating apparently takes place before or during the migration from the cooler climates. The leatherback's shell is actually quite delicate. If the shell is scratched, the animal may bleed. Blood, of course, is the world's best known shark attractant.

Apparently to restrict crawling distance on land and the chances of scratching its shell, leatherbacks tend to prefer steeply graded beaches with deep water approaches. Such conditions allow an unimpeded short crawl in and out.

The Mexican government has protected the Kemp's ridley at Rancho Nuevo since the 1970s. Peter Pritchard

You'll be extremely fortunate to ever see a nesting leatherback: records report only between 38 and 188 leatherback nests annually in Florida. The major nesting sites are in New Guinea, Central America, the Mexican Pacific coast, and the Guianas, especially Surinam and French Guiana.

As to be expected, leatherback hatchlings are the largest of the sea turtle lot, but not by much: 2-1/2 inches compared to the two-inch hatchlings of loggerheads and greens.

Kemp's Ridley

The Kemp's ridley is sometimes mistaken for a loggerhead, but there are some important shell differences that become quite obvious when you look for them.

43

SEA TURTLES

Like the loggerhead, Kemp's ridley has five pairs of costal plates on the back but rarely more. More importantly, the Kemp's carapace is often as wide as it is long; loggerhead shells are somewhat oval-shaped, like a shield, except they narrow at the back.

One important difference is the one you're least likely to see since it's on the turtle's underside (plastron). Kemp's ridley generally has four (although occasionally three) inframarginal scutes separating the main plastral scutes from the marginal scutes. Furthermore, each inframarginal scute on the Kemp's ridley has a single pore near the posterior border; the loggerhead lacks such pores.

Another telling feature: ridleys are small. Adult Kemp's ridleys weigh between 85 and 100 pounds. The carapace is dark gray or grayish-brown in the young, olive green in adults.

Kemp's ridley is considered the rarest and most endangered of all the sea turtles. In the U.S., juveniles and subadults range from Texas to Maine but they are unknown on the Pacific coast. A carnivore, it's favorite food is blue crabs, but it also eats jellyfish, clams, fish and mussels. It is estimated to take between seven and 15 years for Kemp's ridleys to mature.

Kemp's ridley is mentioned in this guide because it is possible you may see the turtle swimming in the water. It is unlikely you will ever see one nest because until recently the only known nesting site was a 20-mile stretch of beach on Mexico's Gulf Coast, about 200 miles south of Brownsville, TX, at Rancho Nuevo.

However, a Kemp's ridley nest was recorded in Florida in the summer of 1994. It is only the second recorded Kemp's ridley nest ever located in Florida; on both occasions

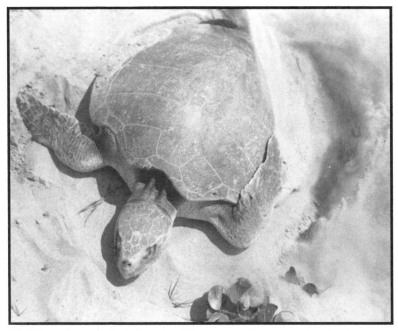

Unlike other sea turtles, the Kemp's ridley nests in the daytime.
Peter Pritchard

the nests were found on Clearwater Beach. In recent years, there have also been one or two nests in the Carolinas.

Mexico's Rancho Nuevo became a protected Natural Reserve in 1977, but by then the Kemp's ridley population had been decimated. From an estimated 40,000 nesting turtles in 1947, the annual nesting number plummeted to fewer than 300 by 1987, although is has now risen to over 500.

Scientists remove the eggs from the nests to beach hatcheries, and they release about 50,000 hatchlings annually. Yet the number of nesting females is very far short of what it should be, a testament to the number of animals accidentally drowned by intensive shrimp trawler activity.

Divers routinely played with hawksbills before the turtles became a protected species.

Kemp's ridley nests in two ways that are unique compared to the sea turtles you might see in Florida.

Both males and females congregate off the beach to mate. The females remain just offshore and crawl onto the beaches only under certain conditions: high surf and strong winds from the northeast between April and June. When there were thousands of them, the females all nested on the beach within hours of each other, then returned to the water. These mass nestings are called arribadas (derived from the Spanish word for arrivals).

Arribadas usually occurred several times a season. What the mysterious cues are that finally lure the Kemp's ridley on to shore, and their significance, are not well understood.

Today, with only a few hundred females left, the arribadas are fitful and small, and many turtles nest singly.

Furthermore, Kemp's ridley nests during the day, not at night as other species usually do.

The Hawksbill

If there was a beauty prize for turtles, the hawksbill would be Miss Universe. Its beautiful shell has always been highly sought for lustrous tortoiseshell jewelry and other ornaments. The carapace is amber-colored with streaks of yellow or reddish and blackish brown. The back shields are translucent when removed from the shell. They also hold a high polish.

The hawksbill is of only modest size: its carapace is normally under three feet and the adults averages 100-120 pounds. Even a turtle of that relatively small size yields up to eight pounds of commercial grade shell. The largest hawksbill ever recorded was a 280-pound animal taken at Grand Cayman.

The hawksbill gained its name from its jaw, although the beak, while certainly bird-like, is not hooked like that of a raptor. All sea turtles have horny beaks, but the hawksbill's head is so narrow that it has a particularly bird-like aspect.

A hawksbill's shell has four pairs of costal scutes but, in contrast to other species, these scutes overlap (except in hatchlings and old adults) and their edges are rough and sharp. The marginal (edge) shields at the posterior are serrated, like a row of saw teeth.

The hawksbill's paddle-shaped front flippers each have two claws and the prefrontal area bears two pairs of scales. The animals mature at about 80 pounds; less in some parts of the Indian and Pacific oceans.

Living throughout the Caribbean, hawksbills are rarely found north of Florida and are scarce even in Florida. The best way to see a hawksbill is during the day: put on a scuba tank and go diving off Palm Beach or Miami, Florida or in the Keys where hawksbills are sometimes found near rocks and coral ledges in depths less than 50 feet.

Hawksbills consume both sea grasses and small animals, but their favorite fare appears to be sponges. Since sponges are composed of numerous small glass-like slivers it's not clear how hawksbills can gain much from, or even tolerate, such a diet. However, for challenging diets, consider the giant leatherback and its watery jellyfish.

Nesting behavior of the hawksbill is generally similar to that of the green turtle, and the two sometimes share nesting beaches. However, hawksbills have the ability to nest where the green and other sea turtles cannot. Hawksbills are able to climb over rocks and other debris that would turn back other species. They move quite briskly on land, and ''walk'' rather than ''lunge forward'' like the heavier green turtles and leatherbacks.

Overall, populations are severely reduced, and hawksbill nests are uncommon. In recent years, they have been found (but very rarely) at the Canaveral National Seashore, in Palm Beach and Martin Counties, south of Port Everglades, and in the Keys.

By necessity, this is a very brief synopsis of hawksbill habits: scientists know less about them than any of the other species that nest within the U.S.

■

3

■

WHY SEA TURTLES
ARE ENDANGERED

If female sea turtles spent their entire lives in the sea, their existence would be far less precarious. Adult turtles are of such a size that they have few natural enemies. The need to bury the eggs on land has always been the sea turtles' greatest vulnerability.

Crawling ashore to nest, sea turtles are defenseless against man. At best, they can move but awkwardly and slowly across a beach. And turtles on land seem to have no real inclination to defend themselves--in contrast to loggerheads or ridleys caught at sea, which may bite vigorously.

A marine turtle on shore has always been a turtle at risk. In the past, large predators such as cougars or jaguars could and did kill nesting turtles. Coastal Indians from North to South America also preyed on turtles for food, both by killing nesting adults and taking the freshly laid eggs.

Historically, hatchlings fresh out of the nest were even more vulnerable than their nesting mothers...perhaps only 1 in 100 or less ever made it to adulthood.

The life of a sea turtle is often a precarious one.

Yet there was a natural balance at work here. As long as the traditional nesting sites were left intact, the turtle population was always able to replace itself. Adults lived many, many years and in a lifetime laid thousands of eggs. The arrival of Europeans is what changed the balance in our part of the world.

Early explorers quickly recognized that sea turtles were an ideal fresh meat source for their sailing voyages. Turtles could be kept alive indefinitely aboard ship by simply rolling the huge creatures on their backs. No special pens, no special feeding arrangements--just stack them up below deck until they were needed. The eggs also provided excellent eating when served fresh, or when dried or smoked in their oviducts.

When sailors were hungry, they could make a quick trip ashore under the cover of darkness, capture a turtle without delay and cook it in its own shell. No muss, no fuss; turtles were the perfect fast food for mariners on the go.

The favorite shipboard species was the green because of its uniformly large size as an adult, its wide distribution throughout the Caribbean, and its delicious flavor.

Not only did British and Spanish vessels fill their holds with turtles while exploring the New World, they brought many home. Eventually, turtles became popular food in Europe. In England, the clear soup made from the green turtle soon became a status symbol at important banquets. Ironically, in the New World, turtles were often served as slave food.

On the island of Bermuda, at least, some protection was afforded sea turtles as early as 1620 when The Bermuda Assembly adopted the following legislation--the first turtle conservation law in the world. What appear to be typos and spelling errors were actually the King's upper crust English of the time:

An Act Agaynst The Killinge of Ouer Young Tortoyses
In regard that much waste and abuse hath been offered and yet it is by sundrye lewd and impvident psons inhabitinge within these Islands who in their continuall goinges out to sea for fish doe upon all occasions, And at all tymes as they can meete them, snatch & catch up indifferently all kinds of Tortoyses both

yonge and old little and greate and soe kill carrye awaye and devoure them to the much decay of the breed of so excellent a fishe the daylye skarringe of them from our shores and the danger of an utter distroyinge and losse of them.

It is therefore enacted by the Authoritie of this present Assembly That from hence forward noe manner of pson or psons of what degree or condition soeuer he be inhabitinge or remayninge at any time within these Islands shall pseume to kill or cause to be killed in any Bay Sound or Harbor or any other place out to Sea: being wthin five leagues** round about of those Islands any young Tortoyses that are or shall not be Eighteen inches in the Breadth or Dyameter and that upon the penaltye for euerye such offence of the fforfeyture of fifteen pounds of Tobacco whereof the one half is to be bestowed in the publique uses the other upon the informer.

(**A league was a measure of distance that varied from 2.4 to 4.6 statute miles.)

The Bermuda colonists living 600 miles off the coast of North Carolina may have been alarmed about the future of their sea turtles, but few other New World residents ever were.

The easiest place to capture large numbers of green turtles were the great rookeries in the Caribbean where turtles were so plentiful that they crawled over each other in search of nesting space. Turtle rookeries were exploited for centuries. Few seemed concerned about tomorrow's turtle supply. What was more important was the number of turtles that could be captured today. The future would take care of itself.

It did. The rookeries were so overharvested that only one mainland green turtle rookery remained by the 1900s: Tortuguero on the coast of Costa Rica. All the others were annihilated or the nesting population reduced to such small numbers it took long searches over considerable stretches of beach to locate just a single turtle.

Once flipped on its back, a sea turtle is helpless.

In the United States, turtles (mostly greens) were commercially harvested in Texas, Louisiana, Virginia, Georgia and North Carolina. However, none came close to comparing with the turtling in Florida during the 1800s and 1900s.

In Florida, turtles were harvested locally and also imported from the Caribbean to supply turtle meat, soup and stew. In-state harvests declined just as dramatically as they did in the Caribbean. For instance, one turtle operation in 1886 reported capturing 2,500 turtles on the east coast in the Indian River district using just eight nets. By 1895,

Turtles could be stored on their back aboard ship for weeks by early New World explorers.

only 60 turtles were taken by the same operation using six nets. Over on Florida's west coast near Tampa in 1895, four nets captured a grand total of only 55 turtles.

However, the population dropped spectacularly before 1895. In 1890, 24 men using 168 nets captured only 738 turtles, less than a third of the 1886 harvest. Yet 1890 was also something of a peak year for turtling when revenues (primarily from greens) totaled $20,972. This amounted to one-fourth of the value of all fishing-related activities in Florida for that year.

The turtle kraals of Key West in the 1940s. This is a male green turtle being dragged on to the dock. Oliver Young

The Keys themselves were also once a great turtling area. Old turtle ''kraals'' where the animals were kept still remain in Key West as a reminder of those days. In the 1900s, fewer and fewer of the turtles were actually captured in the Keys--there simply weren't that many left--but were imported from Nicaragua and Costa Rica by the Cayman Islands turtle fleet, who long ago had exterminated their own turtles. Until the 1970s, turtle soup was still canned in the Keys and shipped around the country. Still, in keeping with the gourmet stature of turtle soup, two other rather unlikely places actually out-produced Key West for a time: New York and London.

SEA TURTLES

Green turtles are raised at the Cayman Turtle Farm.

On the Caribbean island of Grand Cayman, green turtles were successively farmed in inland tanks in order to supply the commercial demand at a time when natural stocks were deteriorating badly. However when the United States banned the import of all turtle products in 1979, regardless of their source, the Cayman Turtle Farm ultimately became mostly a tourist attraction. Yet, it does supply turtle meat for the Cayman Islands and even makes a modest profit.

Traditionally, a harvested sea turtle was an amazingly versatile source of food and decoration. Green turtles were the most sought for meat, which came from the body muscle and the flippers. These typically amounted to around 40 percent of the total body weight. The prized clear soup came from the cartilaginous parts of the shell. Oil from green turtles was also touted as a cosmetic for a time, while the skin was used to replace the leather of other endangered reptile species such as alligator and crocodile.

As table fare, hawksbills had a Russian roulette reputation. Generally tasty, and occasionally even preferred to the green turtle, yet at certain times and places hawksbills

By nature, green turtles are not aggressive toward humans.

were reported to be poisonous. So local fishermen would feed the turtle's liver to the crows to test its fitness.

But a hawksbill shell was always a great prize. In young hawksbills, the scutes (or scales) initially overlap, then become juxtaposed as the animal ages. It is the overlapping shell (thicker than the smooth shell of older animals) that was most highly prized for decoration. The shell, easily separated in boiling water so the scutes could be removed, was used in fashioning knife handles, ear rings and other ornamental accessories.

On Florida's west coast, the meat and eggs from both loggerhead and green turtles were popular for decades among residents, although much of the loggerhead meat was sold as green turtle.

Leatherbacks were never used commercially for meat or decoration, but the eggs were intensively harvested. Leatherback meat was edible but too oily for most palates-- except those who were truly hungry.

PHOTO ESSAY

In some parts of the world today, turtle meat is an important source of food and income. In Nicaragua, for instance, the Mosquito Indians must travel many miles through rough seas to capture green turtles feeding far offshore.

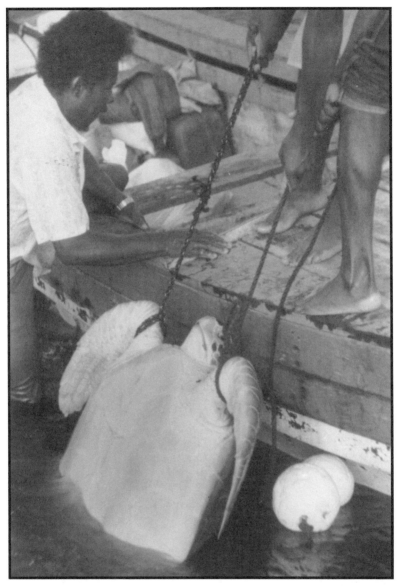

Hoisting 300 pounds of green turtle turtle aboard a fishing boat in the Mosquito Keys is not easy.

Although the children there might sometimes play with a turtle...

...they also keep them in good health until the animal is slaughtered.

Shade trees supply the only refrigeration.

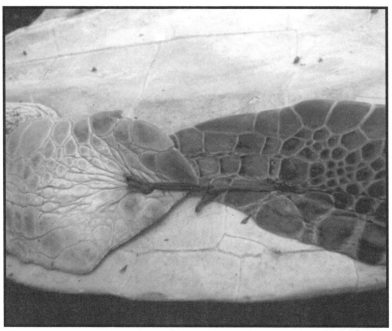

To keep the turtles from slapping, their flippers are perforated and tied.

These male green turtles will be slaughtered after midnight so the meat will be fresh for the town market, which opens at dawn.

63

The Indians allow researchers to conduct studies on a turtle before cleaning.

Afterwards, the shells are gathered and burned.

Protective Legislation

Currently, the Federal Endangered Species Act lists the hawksbill, leatherback and Kemp's ridley as endangered species. The green turtle is considered endangered in Florida and on the Pacific coast of Mexico only; it is regarded as a threatened species elsewhere. The loggerhead is considered a threatened species.

It is illegal to sell or import into the United States any marine turtle products without a permit authorizing import for conservation or scientific purposes. But because sea turtles either live in or migrate into the waters of many nations, they need the safety provided by international treaties for true and lasting protection. Several such treaties do exist, but not all countries are signatories; those that are not, such as Japan, continue to import substantial quantities of turtle products. Even in those countries where the capture and sale of turtles are banned, enforcement of the law may be severely limited by lack of funding--or lack of real commitment.

In 1994, Florida voters took an important step to protect sea turtles by passing an amendment to their state constitution which bans the use of fishing nets in coastal waters. In recent years, such nets have probably accounted for more deaths of green turtles in Florida than any other single factor.

The Problem of "Night Lights"

Inadvertently, people are still causing the deaths of many marine turtle hatchlings because of the many artificial light sources we humans require to see in the dark--or insist on being utilized when we are not even present. These include porch and pool lights, street lights, illuminated street signs and parking lots, car headlights, bug zappers and security spotlights. Even interior lights visible through home windows can be a problem for hatchlings.

As mentioned previously, hatchlings wait below the surface until dark before making their dash to the sea. Perhaps the most important cue for guiding them in the proper direction is the inborn trait to go where it's brightest. Normally, even on a dark night, that would be the water. Hatchlings instinctively avoid darkly silhouetted objects, such as vegetation and sand dunes, which are generally situated in the direction away from the sea.

Under totally natural conditions, the brightest region (regardless of moon phase) is the ocean reflecting the night sky. Nearby street lights and porch lights, far brighter than any distant ocean reflection, can draw hatchlings like moths, and the results are often fatal.

Hatchlings attempting to cross roads to reach street lights may be crushed by cars or become so totally disoriented

SEA TURTLES

These Kemp's ridley will be placed in a hatchery to ensure nesting success. The eggs are caught in a plastic bas as the turtle deposits them. Peter Pritchard

they travel far away from the ocean, where they become easy prey at dawn.

For this reason, many Florida communities now have strict ordinances regulating beach-front lighting near nesting areas from June through October.

If you are walking a public beach at night and happen to encounter wayward hatchlings, experts advise you should take them to a darkened part of the beach and permit them to complete their journey to the sea. Hatchlings are notorious for their energetic crawling once out of the nest: if you encounter turtles who display very little activity, place them in the ocean to help them swim away.

Also call the Florida Marine Patrol toll free at 1-800-DIAL-FMP and alert them to what you've encountered. If the situation seems serious enough, they can dispatch someone to oversee and manage the problem.

Although misdirection occurs more commonly for hatchlings, any light seen from the surf has the potential to misdirect a turtle, including the adults coming ashore to nest.

Barriers To Successful Nesting

Some parts of Florida where sea turtles once nested are off limits today because of altered conditions. For instance, sea walls and erosion-control structures literally wall off the beach.

In places where there is still open access, the introduction of exotic vegetation, particularly Australian pines, makes former nesting sites unsuitable because of their system of interlocking roots which make nest digging impossible. Furthermore, the trees also shade out the sun, and a lower incubation temperature may prevent the hatchlings from developing properly, or may produce mainly or only male hatchlings.

Other important deterrents:

• Turtles tend to concentrate near shore during the nesting season. They also tend to rest or travel near or just under the surface where boat and jet ski ("personal watercraft") operators may not be able to see them to avoid a collision.

• Off-road vehicles or horses on a nesting beach may cause nests to collapse.

• Hurricanes or heavy rains can flood sea turtle nests, drowning the eggs.

SEA TURTLES

Turtles must nest above the high water line.

- Discarded monofilament line, untended fishing traps and nets may cause fatalities if the turtles become entangled in the gear and drown.
- In South Florida, beach restoration sometimes makes it impossible for sea turtles to excavate their nests. The soft loamy sand traditionally found in places like Broward County is commonly being replaced by sand with clay

particles that may "bake" to a hardness impossible for the turtles to dig through.

• In some areas, the raccoon population is unnaturally high in that the raccoons have no predators, are not hunted and they can raid the trash cans when food is scarce. Raccoons are notorious for eating turtle eggs and destroying the nests. In the recent past, raccoons were credited with destroying almost all the nests on some Central Florida beaches.

• Floating debris is sometimes mistaken for food and eaten. Plastic bags and balloons are similar to jellyfish in shape and texture and jellyfish are a normal part of certain sea turtles' diets. Unfortunately, the plastic becomes an obstruction in the turtle's gut, prevents normal food absorption and results in death. It is now illegal for vessels to dump plastic trash in the ocean or the territorial waters of the United States.

While plastic garbage bags and bottles are the most obvious problems, sea turtles and other wildlife may even die after eating the most innocent of items: the remains of helium-filled Mylar balloons, released by the hundreds of thousands at theme parks, festivals and outdoor sporting events. The release of such balloons outdoors is now limited by Florida law to 10 within any 24-hour period.

SEA TURTLES

■

4

■

THE NESTING PROCESS
IN DETAIL

Although nesting occurs during different months of the year in other parts of the world, Florida's main nesting season is from the end of May through September. Considerable information has been gathered about the nesting process, since it is one of the few aspects of a sea turtle's life than can be easily observed.

The nesting behavior of all sea turtle species is essentially the same, although there may be some minor variations. Carr and Ogren, who gave the first detailed description of the events, broke the process down into 11 different stages. The process has been recorded as lasting as little as a single hour and, in rare cases, as long as seven. Between one and two hours is considered the norm.

1. Stranding, testing of the stranding site, and emerging from the wave wash. Stranding refers to the turtle entering water so shallow that she rests on the bottom rather than floats. Typically, when a turtle first emerges from the water, she will stop to press the stand with her nose as if smelling or otherwise evaluating the texture. The ''sand smelling'' is probably for the detection of the abrupt thermal gradient that tells the turtle she is now above the high tide line.

2. Selecting a course and crawling from the surf to the nesting site. Turtles are at an extreme disadvantage on land since they normally have water buoyancy to support them as they breathe. On shore, their weight tends to compress the lungs, which makes it difficult for them to breathe. While slowly crawling to the nesting site, the turtle will often raise its head as if looking around.

Note: at this stage, as well as when the turtle is first emerging from the water, lights or motion will often cause the turtle to return to the water. It still might come ashore a few hours later at another point on the beach, or it might postpone nesting for a night or two.

3. Selection of nesting site. Turtles nest well above the tideline. Otherwise, excessive dampness or standing water will cause the eggs to deteriorate and the embryos will die.

4. Clearing of nest area. Once having reached a suitable spot, a turtle will use its fore flippers to scoop out a shallow ''body pit.'' The hind flippers flip sand away from the area that will be excavated for the egg cavity. The track of a turtle that comes ashore and departs without any attempt at nesting is known as a ''false crawl.''

Turtles will sometimes end their nest building and return to the water for any of the following reasons:

a) obstruction of the digging by thick tree roots, rocks or logs which make digging difficult or impossible.

b) the sides of the nesting chamber collapsing because the sand is too dry to maintain a steep-walled configuration.

c) interruption by other turtles, animals or humans.

5. Excavating the body pit. Only the hind limbs are used to dig the egg chamber. If a turtle nesting late in the season happens to choose a site close to where other eggs

PHOTO ESSAY

This loggerhead is excavating her body pit.

Sand gets thrown everywhere during the excavation process.

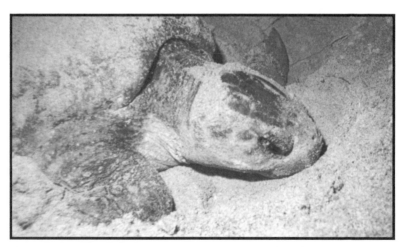

Once a sea turtle begins excavating seriously, she rarely stops.

The back flippers carefully dig the nest hole.

In order to keep the nest hole from collapsing, the female turtle has to work delicately.

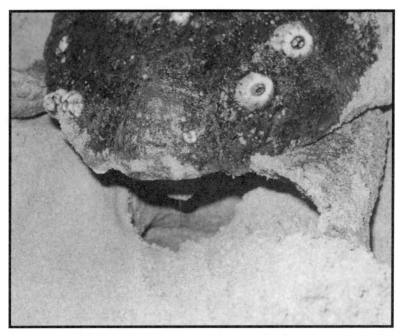

Here she folds her flippers out of the way before depositing the eggs.

Now she begins depositing her eggs, laying as many as 100 in a single clutch.

The eggs often drop with a considerable amount of mucus.

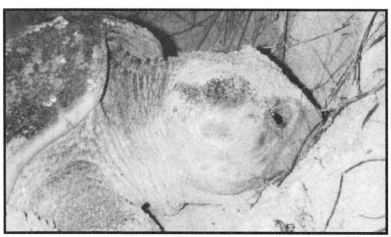

Tears during the nesting process serve to remove sand from the surface of the eye.

Once the eggs are laid, she covers her nest...

are already incubating, she literally thinks nothing of disturbing or wrecking the earlier clutch as she digs a fresh pit. Gulls and other predators will feed on the excavated eggs, effectively destroying the first nest. And the spilled yolk will contaminate the new eggs, preventing their hatching also.

Even if the disturbed eggs are replanted by human help, the eggs often do not hatch.

...and returns to the sea.

6. Excavating the nest hole. The completed nest hole averages about 18 inches deep, roughly 10 inches in diameter and is bottle shaped. The female is able to dig deeply by raising her head and pushing up with the fore flippers. This slanting position permits the hind flippers to dig deeper. In order to keep the nest hole from collapsing, the hind flippers work as delicate scoops to remove the sand, which is thrown backward and away from the hole, just before the flipper is re-inserted.

SEA TURTLES

Something the mother never sees: her hatchlings. This is a leatherback. Peter Pritchard

7. **Oviposition.** After she folds her flippers out of the way, the female will deposit, on average, about 100 eggs. The eggs drop two or three at a time, along with considerable mucus, from the cloaca. At this point almost nothing will stop a turtle from depositing her eggs, not even a raccoon catching and eating the eggs as they drop.

Note the nesting turtle's eyes, which will probably have tears in them. At one time it was believed these tears resulted from pain or the exertion of the egg laying process. Not so. Sea turtles shed such tears continuously in order to rid their bodies of excess salts. The large glands responsible for these salty secretions are located behind the eyes.

Sea turtle eggs are white and spherical, measuring from 40 to 60 mm in diameter. They also are soft and may appear slightly dented when initially laid. This dent disappears after a few days. At first, the yolk of newly laid eggs is undifferentiated protein, oil and water. But the embryo is visible at 10 days, and the heart is beating and the eye is well advanced. The development of the eggs of a particular clutch is fairly uniform. Sunlight and weather are important factors determining incubation time, which is why turtles select the summer months for nesting in temperate regions. From 55 to 60 days is the normal incubation period for Florida.

8. Filling, covering and packing of nest hole. The hind flippers are used to fill in the nesting hole.

9. Filling of body pit and concealing of nesting site. The female uses both foreflippers (or one foreflipper and the opposite hind flipper) to scatter sand in all directions in an attempt to disguise the nesting site.

10. Selecting a course and returning to the sea. The female will continue to scatter sand in all directions as she returns to the water, apparently to hide the nest's location. However, the turtle's tread-like tracks are anything but inconspicuous to those who know what to look for.

11. Re-entry to the sea. The turtle enters the water, pushing off the bottom until she is able to float, and swims away.

Multiple nesting: Once is not enough. It's possible the same female will return to the same or to other sections of the beach to nest again later the same season. Greens, loggerheads and hawksbills tend to renest in 12 to 15 days while leatherbacks wait only nine or 10 days.

SEA TURTLES

■

5

■

WHERE TO SEE
NESTING TURTLES

Because sea turtles are endangered or threatened species, people taking part in organized turtle watches in the United States are subject to various federal and state laws. Anyone conducting a turtle walk in Florida must have a permit from the Florida Department of Environmental Protection (407/575-5407). Touching a sea turtle or handling its eggs without a permit is unlawful.

These are the current guidelines that those conducting and participating in turtle watches must follow. They provide an excellent description of what you will and will not see on a turtle watch. In essence, you're allowed to approach a turtle only after she's started laying her eggs.

Turtle Watch Guidelines
Florida Department of Environmental Protection

● Turtle watches may be conducted only with loggerhead turtles (which are classified as threatened, not endangered). If any other species is encountered on the nesting beach, the group cannot be guided to that area.

● Interpretive programs (lectures, slide presentations, etc.) which incorporate updated information on sea turtle

This leatherback did not complete her nesting before sunrise.
Peter Pritchard

conservation and biology are mandatory. Programs should be presented prior to the actual watch and must include an explanation of procedures to be followed during the turtle watching experience.

- Group size should not exceed 25 people per guide, with the total group not to exceed 50 persons. All guides must be thoroughly trained and listed on the Marine Turtle Permit issued by the Florida Department of Environmental Protection.

- Public awareness turtle watches may not be conducted for profit or exploited for commercial purposes. Fees may be charged only by non-profit organizations to cover legitimate costs incurred in sea turtle conservation efforts. Anyone who charges a fee is subject to litigation and is advised to carry liability insurance.

• Age limitations for participants are left to the discretion of the permit holder.

• Scouts are to be utilized to search for a nesting loggerhead unless the group does not exceed five persons. If an all terrain vehicle (ATV) is used for scouting, a red filter must be placed over the headlights. The headlight can be used only if absolutely necessary, and the ATV must be operated near the water's edge.

• Participants may not use their own flashlights. The use of low intensity flashlights is limited to the walk leader and scouts only. Leaders and scouts may not use flashlights while scouting for a turtle or while conducting participants to the nesting site. A flashlight may be used only to ensure safety while gaining access to the beach.

After approaching the turtle, one light may be used by the group leader or a scout to illuminate the nest cavity so that participants may watch the eggs being deposited. The light may not be turned on the turtle until after she has started covering her nest. Remember that other turtles may be in the area, and hatchlings may be emerging nearby. Improper use of a light can deter nesting turtles and/or disorient emergent hatchlings.

• Turtle watch leaders and scouts are encouraged to invite persons who are out on their own looking for turtles to join the group. This is an opportunity to educate persons who might otherwise disturb nesting turtles.

• A leader or scout must exercise great caution when exposing the nest so as not to disturb the turtle. Exposing the nest must be conducted prior to the group's arrival at the nesting site. At no time should sand be allowed to fall into the nesting chamber.

SEA TURTLES

- Participants must stay with their group and remain at all times. The group may not approach the turtle until egg deposition is well underway. Participants, scouts, and the leader must approach from the rear and remain behind the nesting turtle while she is laying her eggs. At the principal permit holder's discretion, a single egg may be removed from the nest and passed around for the participants to touch. The egg must be returned to the nest before the turtle finishes laying its eggs.
- Contact (light touching) with the nesting female is permitted only after all the eggs have been deposited. Contact must not impede nest covering or the turtle's return to the ocean.
- Flash photography and lights for filming are not permitted.
- Only one nesting turtle is to be observed by the group each night.
- No more than four turtle watches per seven-day week may be conducted in the selected beach area.
- Public turtle watches may not be conducted in the following area because of its special significance as an ongoing research site: The Melbourne Beach area from the north boundary of Sebastian Inlet State Park north to the south border of Spessard Holland Park.

The Archie Carr National Wildlife Refuge is in the process of being established on the stretch of beach between Melbourne and Wabasso, which includes Brevard and Indian River Counties. Targeted to protect 860 acres of barrier islands, this is the country's first and only turtle preserve. It is named after the world renowned sea turtle researcher who helped found the Caribbean Conservation Corporation.

The Archie Carr NWR attracts more nesting loggerheads (a threatened species) than anywhere else in the world, except for Masirah Island (Oman). Leatherbacks and green turtles (both endangered) nest here more commonly than anywhere else in the nation.

The Turtle Watchers
Florida

All of the turtle walk programs are on Florida's East Coast since this is where the greatest concentration of nesting occurs. You are not allowed to use a flashlight or take flash photography. For pictures of the egg laying--which you generally are permitted to photograph but verify this ahead of time--you will need fast film and a tripod. At night, even fast film is unlikely to work.

The guides always do their best to find a turtle, but since sea turtles are wild animals with minds of their own, there are no guarantees.

Canaveral National Seashore/
Merritt Island National Wildlife Refuge

• Walks are jointly conducted by the U.S. Fish and Wildlife Service (which has jurisdiction over the Merritt Island NWR) and the National Park Service (which has jurisdiction over Canaveral National Seashore). The programs start at 8PM and last until midnight. If a turtle is not sighted by 11PM, the walk is canceled.

• Walks are held at both the north and southern ends of Canaveral National Seashore. In the northern section, participants assemble at the Canaveral National Seashore Information Center, 7611 South Atlantic Avenue, New Smyrna Beach.

• Southern walks depart from the Merritt Island National Wildlife Refuge Visitor Information Center, five

SEA TURTLES

miles east of Titusville on State Road 406. Traditionally, more walks are held at the southern end.

● Reservations for the northern section are made by calling the Canaveral Information Center 904/428-3384. Calls are taken May 15 for the June walks; on June 15 for the July turtle watches.

● Reservations for the southern district are taken on May 15 for both the June and July programs.

● Merritt Island National Wildlife Refuge takes all of its turtle walk reservations on a single day in early May. Call 407/861-0667 in late April to find out which day in May.

● Both the northern and southern districts of the seashore each have a road five miles long with boardwalks at various intervals. Turtles are observed within one-quarter of a mile of a boardwalk.

● Groups are limited to 25 per watch. The age limit is 8 years old.

Orlando Science Center
743 West Winter Park Street, Orlando

● As part of its Summer Adventure Series, the Science Center in land-locked Orlando offers turtle walks on Friday and Saturday evenings in June and July.

● Classes are limited to 20 and begin in mid-June. For information/enrollment, call the Orlando Science Center at 407/896-7151.

● Class members meet at the Science Center at 6PM for an orientation and lecture that lasts between one and two hours. Even if it rains, class members should still attend their session so an alternate time for the walk can be scheduled.

Studies have been conducted along Canaveral National Seashore beaches since the 1970s.

• Following the educational presentation, class members car pool to Melbourne Beach where the actual turtle walk is held. In order to allow enough time for

SEA TURTLES

everyone to stop for dinner on the way, the turtle walk doesn't begin until 10PM. It ends according to when a turtle is found.

Since the Melbourne area is the largest nesting area of loggerhead turtles in the Western Hemisphere, the chances of seeing a turtle are unusually good.

Sea Turtle Preservation Society
Melbourne Beach

● Turtle walks are conducted by this organization in June and July. However, the society did not supply any further information. The contact number is 407/676-1701.

Sebastian Inlet State Recreation Area
9700 South A1A
Melbourne Beach, FL 32951

● Public walks are conducted Friday, Saturday, Sunday and Monday nights of June and July.

● Reservations are taken two weeks ahead of a scheduled walk. The first call of the day is taken at 9AM. Groups are limited to 20 people.

● Telephone 407/589-2147. You can make reservations for up to six people.

● Assemble at the McLarty Treasure Museum at 9PM for orientation and a sea turtle presentation. The McLarty Museum is two miles south of the Sebastian Inlet Bridge on A1A. Scouts will be looking for a nesting turtle during the program.

● The program is conducted in almost all weather conditions unless lightning is present. The recommended minimum age limit is 8 years old. The beach walk could be up to three miles long. The program ends at midnight.

Note the ridges on the center scutes of this immature loggerhead.

Florida Power & Light
Hutchinson Island

Florida Power & Light is a nationally recognized leader in helping protect the state's plants and wildlife, particularly manatees and sea turtles.

SEA TURTLES

● Walks are conducted Wednesday, Friday and Saturday evenings at the FPL St. Lucie Nuclear Power Plant on Hutchinson Island.

● Reservations are made by calling (in Florida only) 800-334-5483 after May 15. Walks begin at 9PM with an orientation and education program.

● Walks are limited to 50 people, who wait in the auditorium until scouts find a nesting loggerhead. Then everyone is taken by truck to the nearest access gate, so only brief walks are normally required to reach the nesting site. Activities usually end by midnight but may last longer if the turtle under observation hasn't completed her nesting.

A limited number of spaces are reserved for guests staying at the three hotels on South Hutchinson Island.

Gumbo Limbo Nature Center
1801 North Ocean Blvd.
Boca Raton

Because of the manner in which the turtle walks are arranged, only area residents generally have an opportunity to join the sea turtle walks held from the end of May until the last week of July.

Instead of taking reservations, the center advertises a single Saturday when turtle walk tickets will go on sale. Normally, all the tickets for the entire season are sold out on that Saturday.

Marinelife Center of Juno Beach
1200 U.S. Hwy. 1, Loggerhead Park, Juno Beach

● Turtle walks are conducted Sunday, Tuesday, Wednesday and Thursday evenings in June and July.

This is a rare photo of a juvenile leatherback. Peter Pritchard

● Reservations may be made beginning May 1 on a first-come basis: 407/627-8280.

● There is a limit of 50 persons per watch, with no restrictions on age.

● The walks cover about 300 yards of beach.

● A donation of $2.50 per person is requested.

Assemble at 9PM at the Loggerhead Park tennis court pavilion, 1200 U.S. Hwy. 1, Juno Beach. If no turtle is sighted by 11:30PM, the watch is ended.

● You don't need to make a night walk to view sea turtles close-up. The Marinelife Center is the only turtle hospital between Orlando and Ft. Lauderdale that cares for sick or injured turtles. Once the turtles are rehabilitated, they are returned to the sea.

SEA TURTLES

John D. MacArthur Beach State Park
10900 State Road 703, North Palm Beach.

- Walks are held Mondays and Thursdays in June and July and last from one to two hours.
- Reservations are taken no sooner than the first working day following Memorial Day: 407/624-6952. Groups are limited to 25.
- Participants first assemble about 8:30 p.m. at the park's nature center for an educational program on sea turtles.
- Participants reassemble on the main dune crossover, about mid-way on the 1.8-mile beach, while scouts are sent to the north and south to locate turtles. Hope for a breeze to keep the mosquitoes down. Sand gnats are sometimes more of a problem.
- The maximum amount of territory covered by walking is under two miles. There are no age restrictions.
- Normal state park admission fees apply: $3.25 for a vehicle holding up to eight people.

John U. Lloyd State Recreation Area
6503 North Ocean Drive, Dania.

- Walks are held Wednesday and Friday evenings in June and July. They last between one and three hours, depending on when a nesting turtle is sighted.
- Reservations are taken beginning May 1 by calling the park at 305/923-2833. Each group is limited to a maximum of 25 people with a minimum age limit of six years old.
- The program begins at 9PM with an orientation and presentation at the park's Educational Facility.

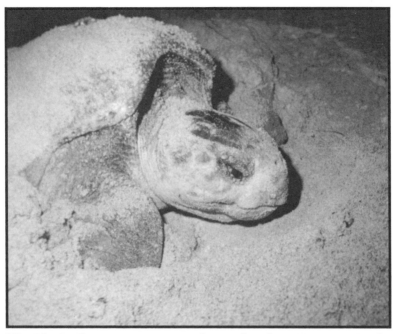

Florida is the most important loggerhead nesting site in the Western Hemisphere.

● You are encouraged to arrive earlier to view the turtle shells and skulls collected over the years. Information brochures are also available.

● The walk covers about a half-mile of beachfront.

Normal state park admission fees apply: $3.25 per vehicle with a maximum of eight people per vehicle.

Hobe Sound Nature Center
Hobe Sound, FL

● Walks are scheduled Tuesday and Thursday evenings in June and July. Walks are usually over by midnight but have been known to last until 1AM.

SEA TURTLES

- Reservations should be made by calling the Nature Center at 407/546-2067 starting in April. Thirty people are allowed to sign up for each walk, with no minimum age restrictions. Waiting lists are also taken in case of last-minute cancellations.

- Participants assemble in the Center's classroom at the Hobe Sound National Wildlife Refuge beginning at 9PM for a 40-minute presentation. The refuge is located on U.S. 1 in southern Martin County.

- After the presentation, participants drive the 5 minutes from the Refuge to Hobe Sound Public Beach. Scouts will have arrived ahead of the group to locate a turtle along a stretch of beach that is approximately one mile in length.

- The actual walk to the turtle is normally less than a half-mile. Participants wait in the relative luxury of a covered pavilion with restrooms and drinking fountain until the scouts locate a turtle.

Donations are requested.

Museum of Discovery and Science
401 Southwest Second Street
Fort Lauderdale

Even if you don't sign up for a turtle walk through the museum, you should still try and visit. During the summer months, a visible nest of live, incubating eggs is on display.

In addition, you have the opportunity to actually touch two of the live display turtles. Both are loggerheads, one a yearling, the other a hatchling. Essentially, these turtles are part of a rotating exhibit since once they mature beyond snack food size, they are released into the wild in their developmental habitat and replaced by younger animals from the visible nest.

Ridley hatchlings run to the sea. Peter Pritchard

The display turtles are not captured specimens but always animals hatched at the museum.

The beach walks, believe it or not, take place in the heart of Fort Lauderdale itself on a stretch of beach where the condo lights are not overpowering. Because this is such a highly developed area, most of the sea turtle nests have to be relocated to hatcheries, which are not open to the public.

• Walks are held once or twice a week during the peak nesting season, between the last two weeks of June and the first two weeks of July.

• Walks are usually held closest to a full moon and high tide, which appear to prompt greater nesting activity in this area. Reservations are taken beginning around April 15: 305/467-6637, ext. 315. Ask for the group tour administrator. Groups are limited to 50.

- Participants assemble at 9PM at the museum for an educational presentation and inspection of the museum's sea turtle exhibits.

- Participants next caravan to the South Beach parking lot across from the Bahia Mar Resort and Marina. Depending on the turtle's location, a walk could cover a maximum of 1.5 miles.

- There is no minimum age limit. Walks normally end by 1AM at the latest.

- A small fee is charged. This money is used to help defray the expenses of the museum's on-going sea turtle displays, which are seen by over 550,000 persons annually.

Blowing Rocks Preserve
Tequesta

- Blowing Rocks Preserve is a unique geologic formation, the largest Anastasia limestone outcropping on the Atlantic Coast. Extending for more than a mile along Jupiter Island, this facility is owned and operated by The Nature Conservancy.

- At this time, turtle walks are by invitation only and are not open to the general public.

Where To See Hatchlings Emerge

Turtle walks show only the nesting process. Few people ever observe the hatchlings emerge at night, under totally natural conditions, and sprint to the water.

You have that chance, ironically, in northwest Florida, an area that does not attract that many sea turtles to begin with. During the month of August and September, the Natural Resources office at Tyndall Air Force Base closely

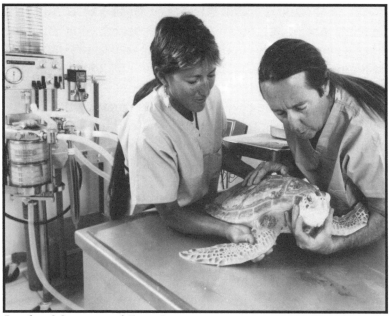

Ritchie Moretti and Tina Brown examine a green turtle at their turtle hospital in Marathon.

monitors the sea turtle nests along its 10 miles of Gulf beach, located about 10 miles east of Panama City. This active military base covers 29,000 acres and is located on a peninsula that abuts the Gulf of Mexico.

A wildlife biologist monitors the beach each day, and whenever it appears that the hatchlings in a particular nest are ready to emerge, the Natural Resources office notifies interested people where to assemble to watch the turtles dig out after dark. By necessity, notice is short, given on the same day when the turtles are expected to emerge. An educational talk by a wildlife biologist accompanies each hatchling watch. Over a season, between three and eight such watches are conducted.

SEA TURTLES

Even though Tyndall Air Force Base has 10 miles of beach, only about 50 nests are recorded each summer. That's very few holes in the sand compared to the thousands of loggerhead nests that may be found on Central Florida's east coast. Because the chances of seeing a turtle crawl are so uncertain, nesting watches are not conducted.

To get on the hatchling watch list, call the Tyndall AFB Natural Resources office at 904/283-2641; or write Natural Resources Office, 325 CES/CEN/42, 119 Alabama Ave., Tyndall Air Force Base, Tyndall, FL 32403.

Where To See Hatchlings Released

"Turtle Time" is an organization that was hatched along the Lee County Coast in 1989. This private, non-profit, all-volunteer organization monitors 12 miles of beach on four islands in the Fort Myers area. Because of the types of beach monitoring and the relative scarcity of nests compared to the Atlantic coast, turtle walks are not conducted. For information, call 813/481-5566.

However, rescued hatchlings which were unable to make it out of the nest on their own are periodically released once six to 10 of the animals have been gathered. The hatchlings are released at night in late June and July.

The World's First Turtle Hospital

Located next to the Hidden Harbor motel in Marathon in the Florida Keys, this hospital specializes in treating green turtles with the disease known as fibropapilloma. This is a disfiguring condition which causes tumors to grow both internally and on the fleshy parts of the turtle's eyes, mouth, neck, flippers, jaw and tail.

Eventually, the tumors may become so big that the tumors blind the turtles, which may cause them to drown or starve. By some estimates, fibropapilloma has infected almost half the green turtles in Florida lagoons. The disease, which became rampant in the 1980s, is believed associated with a virus.

The Hidden Harbor Environmental Project, outfitted with a sterilized operating room, has complete surgical facilities for treating and caring for afflicted turtles. Often as many as 50 green turtles are in residence. They share one of the motel swimming pools with fish and other creatures normally found on the reef to provide the turtles company.

The hospital is not open to the general public. With advance notice, however, special group tours may be arranged through either Tina Brown or Richie Moretti, who founded the world's first turtle medical center:305/743-6509 (the hospital) or 305/743-5376 (Hidden Harbor Motel). Motel guests may also be taken on tours and asked to assist at the hospital, which is located in what once was a lounge for exotic dancers.

Sea Turtle Rehabilitation Facilities

The following have sea turtle rehabilitation facilities:

- Miami Seaquarium
- Marinelife Center of Juno Beach
- Mote Marine Lab, Sarasota
- Sea World of Florida, Orlando
- Marineland of Florida, between Daytona and St. Augustine
- The Gulfarium, Destin
- Gulf World, Panama City

SEA TURTLES

■

6

■

HOW YOU CAN HELP

If sea turtles are to survive into the future--and not just barely cling onto life as endangered to threatened species-- more needs to be done to protect them.

Here are several ways you can help:

Florida Audubon Society

The Florida Audubon Society long has been a leader in sea turtle protection and education in the United States as well as those Central and South American countries hosting large nesting populations. Florida Audubon's turtle expertise is ranked among the nation's best. Donations to Florida Audubon may be restricted to turtle research and education, and should be so stated at the time of donation. For further information, call 407/260-8300. The address is Florida Audubon Society, 460 State Road 436, Casselberry, FL 32707.

Sea Turtle Survival League

This is a program sponsored by the non-profit Caribbean Conservation Corporation, founded in 1959 to help support the work of the late Dr. Archie Carr. The Sea Turtle Survival League hopes to create greater public interest in preserving sea turtles by personalizing them more. For a $25 tax-deductible donation, the League will send you (or

Measuring a rare Kemp's ridley in Mexico. Sea turtle research projects require wide financial support. Peter Pritchard

to anyone you designate) a turtle adoption certificate, a sea turtle fact sheet, a personal profile about your turtle, a decal, and a one-year subscription to the League's quarterly publication. To adopt a sea turtle or to learn more, call 800/ 678-7853.

Marine Turtle Protection Trust Fund

For each donation of $5 or more, the Marine Turtle Protection Trust Fund, Office of Protected Species Management, 3900 Commonwealth Ave., Tallahassee, FL 32399 will provide a color sticker or poster of either a loggerhead or hawksbill turtle. Please specify which you desire.

SEA TURTLES

APPENDICES

SEA TURTLES

APPENDIX A

Turtle Nesting Log

Date _____ Moon Phase_____

Location_____ Tide_____

Weather/Wind Conditions_____

Observed species_____Time _____

For how long_____

Observations_____

_____

_____

Date _____ Moon Phase_____

Location_____ Tide_____

Weather/Wind Conditions_____

Observed species_____Time _____

For how long_____

Observations_____

_____

_____

Date _____ Moon Phase_____

Location_____ Tide_____

Weather/Wind Conditions_____

Observed species_____Time _____

For how long_____

Observations_____

_____

_____

SEA TURTLES

Turtle Nesting Log

Date _____ Moon Phase_____
Location_____ Tide_____
Weather/Wind Conditions_____
Observed species_____Time _____
For how long_____
Observations_____
_____
_____

Date _____ Moon Phase_____
Location_____ Tide_____
Weather/Wind Conditions_____
Observed species_____Time _____
For how long_____
Observations_____
_____
_____

Date _____ Moon Phase_____
Location_____ Tide_____
Weather/Wind Conditions_____
Observed species_____Time _____
For how long_____
Observations_____
_____
_____

Turtle Nesting Log

Date _____ Moon Phase_____
Location_____ Tide_____
Weather/Wind Conditions_____
Observed species_____Time _____
For how long_____
Observations_____
_____
_____

Date _____ Moon Phase_____
Location_____ Tide_____
Weather/Wind Conditions_____
Observed species_____Time _____
For how long_____
Observations_____
_____
_____

Date _____ Moon Phase_____
Location_____ Tide_____
Weather/Wind Conditions_____
Observed species_____Time _____
For how long_____
Observations_____
_____
_____

Turtle Nesting Log

Date _____ Moon Phase _____
Location _____ Tide _____
Weather/Wind Conditions _____
Observed species _____ Time _____
For how long _____
Observations _____
_____
_____

Date _____ Moon Phase _____
Location _____ Tide _____
Weather/Wind Conditions _____
Observed species _____ Time _____
For how long _____
Observations _____
_____
_____

Date _____ Moon Phase _____
Location _____ Tide _____
Weather/Wind Conditions _____
Observed species _____ Time _____
For how long _____
Observations _____
_____
_____

APPENDIX B

Selected Reading

The Sea Turtle: So Excellent a Fishe, Archie Carr, 1986, Austin, TX; U of T Press

Decline of Sea Turtles: Cause and Prevention, National Research Council, 1990, Washington, D.C.; National Academy Press

The Effects of Beach Restoration on Marine Turtles Nesting in South Brevard County, Florida; Paul W. Raymond, 1984, Thesis (M.S.) U.C.F.-Orlando

Movements and Feeding Ecology of Immature Green Turtles, Mary T. Mendonoa, 1981, Thesis (M.S.) U.C.F.-Orlando

A Review of Information on the Subsistence Use of Green and Hawksbill Sea Turtles on Island under U.S. Jurisdiction in the Western Pacific Ocean, R.E. Johannes, 1986, Terminal Island, CA; Southwest Region, National Marine Fisheries Services

Sea Turtles:Natural History and Conservation, Robert Bustard, 1972, New York; Taplinger Publishing Company

Time of the Turtle, Jack Rudloe, 1979, New York; KNOPF; distributed by Random House

The 5 Sea Turtle Species of the U.S. Atlantic and Gulf of the U.S. National Oceanic & Atmospheric Administration, 1985, Washington, D.C.; U.S. Fish & Wildlife Services

Species Composition and Size Class Distribution of Marine Strandings on the Gulf of Mexico & Southeast U.S. Coasts, Wendy Teas, 1985 to 1991 (microform), Miami, FL; U.S. Department of Commerce, Southeast Fisheries Science Center

SEA TURTLES

Selected Reading (cont'd)

Florida Sea Turtles, Van Meter, Victoria Brook, 1983, Miami, FL; Florida Power and Light Company

Encyclopedia of Turtles, Peter C.H. Pritchard, 1979, TFH Publications, Neptune, N.J.

The Ecology and Migration of Sea Turtles, A.Carr and L.Ogren, 1960, Bulletin of the American Museum of Natural History, 121:1-48

Threatened and Endangered Species of the Kennedy Space Center: Marine Turtle Studies, L.M.Ehrhart, 1980, NASA Contract Report 163122

Larsen's Outdoor Publishing
OUTDOORS/NATURE
RESOURCE DIRECTORY

If you are interested in more productive fishing, hunting and diving trips, this information is for you!

Learn how to be more successful on your next outdoor venture from these secrets, tips and tactics. Larsen's Outdoor Publishing offers informational-type books that focus on how and where to catch the most popular sport fish, hunt the most popular game or travel to productive or exciting destinations.

The perfect-bound, soft-cover books include numerous illustrative graphics, line drawings, maps and photographs. Many of our **LIBRARIES** are nationwide in scope. Others cover the Gulf and Atlantic coasts from Florida to Texas to Maryland and some foreign waters. One **SERIES** focuses on the top lakes, rivers and creeks in the nation's most visited largemouth bass fishing state.

> ### THANKS!
> *"I appreciate the research you've done to enhance the sport for weekend anglers."*
> *R. Willis, Jacksonville, FL*

All series appeal to outdoors readers of all skill levels. Their unique four-color cover design, interior layout, quality, information content and economical price makes these books your best source of knowledge. **Best of all, you will know how to be more successful in your outdoor endeavors!!**

ON VIDEO!
Lowrance Electronics Presents
ADVANCED
BASS FISHING
TACTICS
with Larry Larsen

(V1) This 50-minute video is dedicated to serious anglers - those who are truly interested in learning more about the sport and in catching more and larger bass each trip. Part I details how to catch more bass from aquatic vegetaion; Part II covers tips to most effectively fish docks & piers; Part III involves trolling strategies for bigger fish, and Part IV outlines using electronics to locate bass in deep waters. Don't miss this informative and entertaining opportunity where Larry shares his knowledge and expertise!

**Great Tips and Tactics
For The Outdoorsmen
of the Nineties!**

BASS SERIES LIBRARY
by Larry Larsen

(BSL1) FOLLOW THE FORAGE - BASS/PREY RELATIONSHIP - Learn how to determine dominant forage in a body of water and catch more bass!

(BSL2) VOL. 2 BETTER BASS ANGLING TECHNIQUES - Learn why one lure or bait is more successful than others and how to use each lure under varying conditions.

(BSL3) BASS PRO STRATEGIES - Professional fishermen know how changes in pH, water level, temperature and color affect bass fishing, and they know how to adapt to weather and topographical variations. Learn from their experience.

(BSL4) BASS LURES - TRICKS & TECHNIQUES - When bass become accustomed to the same artificials and presentations seen over and over again, they become harder to catch. You will learn how to modify your lures and rigs and how to develop new presentation and retrieve methods to spark the interest of largemouth!

(BSL5) SHALLOW WATER BASS - Bass spend 90% of their time in waters less than 15 feet deep. Learn productive new tactics that you can apply in marshes, estuaries, reservoirs, lakes, creeks and small ponds, and you'll triple your results!

> **HAVE THEM ALL!**
> *"Larry, I'm ordering one book to give a friend for his birthday and your two new ones. I have all the BASS SERIES LIBRARY except one, otherwise I would have ordered an autographed set. I have followed your writings for years and consider them the best of the best!"*
> J. Vinson, Cataula, GA

(BSL6) BASS FISHING FACTS - Learn why and how bass behave during pre- and post-spawn, how they utilize their senses when active and how they respond to their environment, and you'll increase your bass angling success!

(BSL7) TROPHY BASS - If you're more interested in wrestling with one or two monster largemouth than with a "panful" of yearlings, then learn what techniques and locations will improve your chances.

(BSL8) ANGLER'S GUIDE TO BASS PATTERNS - Catch bass every time out by learning how to develop a productive pattern quickly and effectively. "Bass Patterns" is a reference source for all anglers, regardless of where they live or their skill level. Learn how to choose the right lure, presentation and habitat under various weather and environmental conditions!

> **TWO TROPHIES!**
> *"By using your techniques and reading your Bass Series Library of books, I was able to catch the two biggest bass I've ever caught!"*
> B. Conley, Cromwell, IN

(BSL9) BASS GUIDE TIPS - Learn secret techniques known only in a certain region or state that often work in waters all around the country. It's this new approach that usually results in excellent bass angling success. Learn how to apply what the country's top guides know!

Nine Great Volumes To Help You Catch More and Larger Bass!

(LB1) LARRY LARSEN ON BASS TACTICS

is the ultimate "how-to" book that focuses on proven productive methods. **Hundreds of highlighted tips and drawings in our LARSEN ON BASS SERIES explain how you**

can catch more and larger bass in waters all around the country. This reference source by America's best known bass fishing writer will be invaluable to both the avid novice and expert angler!

(PF1) PEACOCK BASS EXPLOSIONS! by Larry Larsen

A must read for those anglers who are interested in catching the world's most exciting fresh water fish! Detailed tips, trip planning and tactics for peacocks in South Florida, Venezuela, Brazil, Puerto Rico, Hawaii and other destinations. This book explores the most effective tactics to take the aggressive peacock bass. You'll learn how to catch

more and larger fish using the valuable information from the author and expert angler, a four-time peacock bass world-record holder. It's the first comprehensive discussion on this wild and colorful fish.

BASS WATERS GUIDE SERIES by Larry Larsen

The most productive bass waters are described in this multi-volume series, including boat ramps, seasonal tactics, water characteristics and more. Numerous maps and photos detail specific locations.

(BW1) GUIDE TO NORTH FLORIDA BASS WATERS - Covers from Orange Lake north and west. Includes Lakes Lochloosa, Talquin and Seminole, the St. Johns, Nassau, Suwannee and Apalachicola Rivers; Newnans Lake, St. Mary's River, Juniper Lake, Ortega River, Lake Jackson, Deer Point Lake, Panhandle Mill Ponds and many more!

(BW2) GUIDE TO CENTRAL FLORIDA BASS WATERS - Covers from Tampa/Orlando to Palatka. Includes Lakes George, Rodman, Monroe, Tarpon and the Harris Chain, the St. Johns, Oklawaha and Withlacoochee Rivers, the Ocala Forest, Crystal River, Hillsborough River, Conway Chain, Homosassa River,

Lake Minneola, Lake Weir, Lake Hart, Spring Runs and many more!

(BW3) GUIDE TO SOUTH FLORIDA BASS WATERS - Covers from I-4 to the Everglades. Includes Lakes Tohopekaliga, Kissimmee, Okeechobee, Poinsett, Tenoroc and Blue Cypress, the Winter Haven Chain, Fellsmere Farm 13. Caloosahatchee River, Lake June-in-Winter, the Everglades, Lake Istokpoga, Peace River, Crooked Lake, Lake Osborne, St. Lucie Canal, Shell Creek, Lake Marian, Lake Pierce, Webb Lake and many more!

OUTDOOR TRAVEL SERIES
by Larry Larsen and M. Timothy O'Keefe

Candid guides on the best charters, time of the year, and other recommendations that can make your next fishing and/or diving trip much more enjoyable.

(OT1) FISH & DIVE THE CARIBBEAN - Vol. 1 Northern Caribbean, including Cozumel, Cayman Islands, Bahamas, Jamaica, Virgin Islands. Required reading for fishing and diving enthusiasts who want to know the most cost-effective means to enjoy these and other Caribbean islands.

(OT3) FISH & DIVE FLORIDA & The Keys - Where and how to plan a vacation to America's most popular fishing and diving destination. Features include artificial reef loran numbers; freshwater springs/caves; coral reefs/barrier islands; gulf stream/passes; inshore flats/channels; and back country estuaries.

> **BEST BOOK CONTENT!**
> *"Fish & Dive the Caribbean" was a finalist in the Best Book Content Category of the National Association of Independent Publishers (NAIP). Over 500 books were submitted by publishers including Simon & Schuster and Turner Publishing. Said the judges "An excellent source book with invaluable instructions. Written by two nationally-known experts who, indeed, know what vacationing can be!"*

DIVING / NATURE SERIES by M. Timothy O'Keefe

(DL1) DIVING TO ADVENTURE shows how to get started in underwater photography, how to use current to your advantage, how to avoid seasickness, how to dive safely after dark, and how to plan a dive vacation, including live-aboard diving.

(DL2) MANATEES - OUR VANISHING MERMAIDS is an in-depth overview of nature's strangest-looking, gentlest animals. They're among America's most endangered mammals. The book covers where to see manatees while diving, why they may be living fossils, their unique life cycle, and much more.

(DL3) SEA TURTLES - THE WATCHERS' GUIDE - Discover how and where you can witness sea turtles nesting in Florida. This book not only gives an excellent overview of sea turtle life, it also provides the specifics of appropriate personal conduct and behavior for human beings on turtle nesting beaches.

(OC1) UNCLE HOMER'S OUTDOOR CHUCKLE BOOK by Homer Circle, Fishing Editor, Sports Afield In his inimitable humorous style, "Uncle Homer" relates jokes, tales, personal anecdotes and experiences covering several decades in the outdoors.

OUTDOOR ADVENTURE by Vin T. Sparano, Outdoor Life

(OA1) HUNTING DANGEROUS GAME - Live the adventure of hunting those dangerous animals that hunt back! Track a rogue elephant, survive a grizzly attack, and face a charging Cape buffalo. These classic tales will make you very nervous next time you're in the woods!

> **KEEP ME UPDATED!**
> *"I would like to get on your mailing list. I really enjoy your books!"*
> G. Granger, Cypress, CA

(OA2) GAME BIRDS & GUN DOGS - A unique collection of tales about hunters, their dogs and the upland game and waterfowl they hunt. You will read about good gun dogs and heart-breaking dogs, but never about bad dogs, because there's no such animal.

COASTAL FISHING GUIDES
by Frank Sargeant

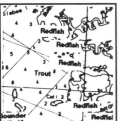

A unique "where-to" series of detailed secret spots for Florida's finest saltwater fishing. These guide books describe hundreds of little-known honeyholes and exactly how to fish them. Prime seasons, baits and lures, marinas and dozens of detailed maps of the prime spots are included. The comprehensive index helps the reader to further pinpoint productive areas and tactics. Over $160 worth of personally-marked NOAA charts in the two books.

(FG1) FRANK SARGEANT'S SECRET SPOTS Tampa Bay to Cedar Key Covers Hillsborough River and Davis Island through the Manatee River, Mullet Key and the Suwannee River.

(FG2) FRANK SARGEANT'S SECRET SPOTS Southwest Florida Covers from Sarasota Bay to Marco.

INSHORE SERIES
by Frank Sargeant

(IL1) THE SNOOK BOOK-"Must" reading for anyone who loves the pursuit of this unique sub-tropic species. Every aspect of how you can find and catch big snook is covered, in all seasons and all waters where snook are found.

(IL2) THE REDFISH BOOK-Packed with expertise from the nation's leading redfish anglers and guides, this book covers every aspect of finding and fooling giant reds. You'll learn secret techniques revealed for the first time. After reading this informative book, you'll catch more redfish on your next trip!

(IL3) THE TARPON BOOK-Find and catch the wily "silver king" along the Gulf Coast, north through the mid-Atlantic, and south along Central and South American coastlines. Numerous experts share their most productive techniques.

(IL4) THE TROUT BOOK -Jammed with tips from the nation's leading trout guides and light tackle anglers. For both the old salt and the rank amateur who pursue the spotted weakfish, or seatrout, throughout the coastal waters of the Gulf and Atlantic.

HUNTING LIBRARY
by John E. Phillips

(DH1) MASTERS' SECRETS OF DEER HUNTING - Increase your deer hunting success by learning from the masters of the sport. New information on tactics and strategies is included in this book, the most comprehensive of its kind.

(DH2) THE SCIENCE OF DEER HUNTING Covers why, where and when a deer moves and deer behavior. Find the answers to many of the toughest deer hunting problems a sportsman ever encounters!

(DH3) MASTERS' SECRETS OF BOW-HUNTING DEER - Learn the skills required to take more bucks with a bow, even during gun season. A must read for those who walk into the woods with a strong bow and a swift shaft.

(DH4) HOW TO TAKE MONSTER BUCKS - Specific techniques that will almost guarantee a trophy buck next season! Includes tactics by some of the nation's most accomplished trophy buck hunters.

> ### RECOMMENDATION!
> *"Masters' Secrets of Turkey Hunting is one of the best books around. If you're looking for a good turkey book, buy it!"* J. Spencer, Stuttgart Daily Leader, AR
>
> ### NO BRAGGIN'!
> *"From anyone else Masters' Secrets of Deer Hunting would be bragging and unbelievable. But not with John Phillips, he's paid his dues!"* F. Snare, Brookville Star, OH

(TH1) MASTERS' SECRETS OF TURKEY HUNTING - Masters of the sport have solved some of the most difficult problems you can encounter while hunting wily longbeards with bows, blackpowder guns and shotguns. Learn the 10 deadly sins of turkey hunting.

(BP1) BLACKPOWDER HUNTING SECRETS - Learn how to take more game during and after the season with black powder guns. If you've been hunting with black powder for years, this book will teach you better tactics to use throughout the year.

FISHING LIBRARY

(CF1) MASTERS' SECRETS OF CRAPPIE FISHING by John E. Phillips Learn how to make crappie start biting again once they have stopped, select the best jig color, find crappie in a cold front, through the ice, or in 100-degree heat. Unusual, productive crappie fishing techniques are included.

(CF2) CRAPPIE TACTICS by Larry Larsen - This book will improve your catch! The book includes some basics for fun fishing, advanced techniques for year 'round crappie and tournament preparation.

> ### CRAPPIE COUP!
> *"After reading your crappie book, I'm ready to overthrow the 'crappie king' at my lakeside housing development!"* R. Knorr, Haines City, FL

(CF3) MASTERS' SECRETS OF CATFISHING by John E. Phillips is your best guide to catching the best-tasting, elusive cats. Learn the best time of the year, the most productive places and which states to fish in your pursuit of Mr. Whiskers.

LARSEN'S OUTDOOR PUBLISHING
CONVENIENT ORDER FORM
ALL PRICES INCLUDE POSTAGE/HANDLING

FRESH WATER
___ BSL1. Better Bass Angling Vol 1 ($12.45)
___ BSL2. Better Bass Angling Vol 2 ($12.45)
___ BSL3. Bass Pro Strategies ($12.45)
___ BSL4. Bass Lures/Techniques ($12.45)
___ BSL5. Shallow Water Bass ($12.45)
___ BSL6. Bass Fishing Facts ($12.45)
___ BSL7. Trophy Bass ($12.45)
___ BSL8. Bass Patterns ($12.45)
___ BSL9. Bass Guide Tips ($12.45)
___ CF1. Mstrs' Scrts/Crappie Fshng ($12.45)
___ CF2. Crappie Tactics ($12.45)
___ CF3. Mstr's Secrets of Catfishing ($12.45)
___ LB1. Larsen on Bass Tactics ($15.45)
___ PF1. Peacock Bass Explosions! ($15.95)

SALT WATER
___ IL1. The Snook Book ($12.45)
___ IL2. The Redfish Book ($12.45)
___ IL3. The Tarpon Book ($12.45)
___ IL4. The Trout Book ($12.45)

OTHER OUTDOORS BOOKS
___ DL1. Diving to Adventure ($12.45)
___ DL2. Manatees/Vanishing ($11.45)
___ DL3. Sea Turtles/Watchers' ($11.45)
___ OC1. Uncle Homer's Outdoor
        Chuckle Book ($9.95)

REGIONAL
___ FG1. Secret Spots-Tampa Bay/
        Cedar Key ($15.45)
___ FG2. Secret Spots - SW Florida ($15.45)
___ BW1. Guide/North Fl. Waters ($14.95)
___ BW2. Guide/Cntral Fl.Waters ($14.95)
___ BW3. Guide/South Fl.Waters ($14.95)
___ OT1. Fish/Dive - Caribbean ($11.95)
___ OT3. Fish/Dive Florida/ Keys ($13.95)

HUNTING
___ DH1. Mstrs' Secrets/ Deer Hunting ($12.45)
___ DH2. Science of Deer Hunting ($12.45)
___ DH3. Mstrs' Secrets/Bowhunting ($12.45)
___ DH4. How to Take Monster Bucks ($13.95)
___ TH1. Mstrs' Secrets/ Turkey Hunting ($12.45)
___ OA1. Hunting Dangerous Game! ($9.95)
___ OA2. Game Birds & Gun Dogs ($9.95)
___ BP1. Blackpowder Hunting Secrets ($14.45)

VIDEO &
SPECIAL DISCOUNT PACKAGES
___ V1 - Video - Advanced Bass Tactics $29.95
___ BSL - Bass Series Library (9 vol. set) $84.45
___ IL - Inshore Library (4 vol. set) $37.95
___ BW - Guides to Bass Waters (3 vols.) $37.95
Volume sets are autographed by each author.

> **BIG MULTI-BOOK DISCOUNT!**
> **2-3 books, SAVE 10%**
> **4 or more books, SAVE20%**

> **INTERNATIONAL ORDERS**
> **Send check in U.S. funds; add $4**
> **more per book for airmail rate**

ALL PRICES INCLUDE POSTAGE/HANDLING

No. of books ___ *x $* ___ *ea = $* ___   *Special Package* ___ *@ $* ___
No. of books ___ *x $* ___ *ea = $* ___   *Video (50-min) $29.95 = $* ___
Multi-book Discount (*%) $* ___   *(Pkgs include discount)= N/A*
    SUBTOTAL 1   *$* ___   *SUBTOTAL 2*   *$* ___

> ___ **For Priority Mail (add $2 more per book)** $ ___
> **TOTAL ENCLOSED (check or money order)** $ ___

NAME _____ *ADDRESS* _____

CITY _____ *STATE* _____ *ZIP* _____

Send check or Money Order to: Larsen's Outdoor Publishing, Dept. RD95
2640 Elizabeth Place, Lakeland, FL 33813 (813)644-3381
(Sorry, no credit card orders)

M.ANATEES

Our Vanishing M.ermaids

This award-winning book is an in-depth overview of nature's strangest-looking, gentlest animals. Manatees are among America's most endangered mammals.

Learn:

- where to see manatees while diving
- why they may be living fossils
- how habitat destruction threatens their survival
- why manatees "kiss"
- their unique life cycle
- why early explorers thought manatees had healing powers...
    ...and much more.

Written by renown author and photographer M. Timothy O'Keefe, the book includes numerous black & white photos illustrating the manatees' behavior.

ORDER TODAY!

INDEX

SEA TURTLES

SEA TURTLES

photograph 89
Pinellas County 16
plastron 29, 30, 33, 44
poachers 15
population 50
pores 44
Port Everglades 48
predators 49, 71, 80
prefrontal scales 30, 33, 47

R

radio tracking devices 23
Rancho Nuevo 38, 44
rarest 44
rehabilitation facilities 95, 103
reproduction 33
rookeries 52

S

Sarasota 38
scutes 29, 93
Sea Turtle Preservation
        Society 92
Sea Turtle Survival League 105
Sea World of Florida 103
Sebastian Inlet State Park 88, 92
South Atlantic 35
South Carolina 30
species 17
speed 20, 41
Spessard Holland Park 88
St. Lucie Nuclear Power
        Plant 94
Surinam 43

T

tagging 20, 25
Tampa 54
tears 82

teeth 18
Texas 44, 53
The Gulfarium 103
tide 26, 74
Titusville 90
Tortuguero 52
tread-like tracks 83
Triassic period 17
turtle conservation law 51
turtle products 58, 66
"Turtle Time" 102
turtle walks 85, 87, 89
turtling 54
Tyndall Air Force Base 100

U

U.S. Fish and Wildlife Service 89

V

vascularization 18
vertebrae 18
vertebral scutes 30
vertebrals 29
vibrations 27
Virginia 16, 53
Volusia County 37
vulnerability 35, 49

W

Wabasso 88
winter range 38